God's Unexpected Blessings

God's Unexpected Blessings

What to Expect From God When You Least Expect It

EDITED BY

Kathy Collard Miller

STARBURST PUBLISHERS

Kathy Collard Miller is the author of 30 books including the best-selling *God's Vitamin "C" for the Spirit* and *God's Abundance*. She speaks across the nation and internationally. Contact: P.O. Box 1058, Placentia, CA 92871. (714) 993-2654. Kathyspeak@aol.com.

To schedule Author appearances write:
Author Appearances, Starburst Promotions, P.O. Box 4123
Lancaster, Pennsylvania 17604 or call (717) 293-0939
www.starburstpublishers.com

CREDITS:
Cover design by David Marty Design
Text design and composition by John Reinhardt Book Design
Illustrations by Melissa A. Burkhart

Unless otherwise noted, or paraphrased by the author, all Scripture quotations are from the New International Version of The Holy Bible.

"Scripture taken from the HOLY BIBLE: NEW INTERNATIONAL VERSION.® NIV.® Copyright© 1973, 1978, 1984 by International Bible Society. Used by permission of Zondervan Publishing House."

"The "NIV" and "New International Version" trademarks are registered in the United States Patent and Trademark Office by International Bible Society."

To the best of its ability, Starburst Publishers has strived to find the source of all material. If there has been an oversight, please contact us and we will make any correction deemed necessary in future printings. We also declare that to the best of our knowledge all material (quoted or not) contained herein is accurate, and we shall not be held liable for the same.

First Printing, April 1998
ISBN: 0-914984-07-1
Library of Congress Catalog Number 97-80889
Printed in the United States of America

Contents

ᵉ§ *Introduction*

O<small>UR AWESOME</small> G<small>OD</small> has the wonderful ability to surprise us! At times, we think we have Him all figured out and then He does something that wasn't expected at all. That's especially evident when His great power takes a difficult time in our lives and brings good from it. And it's just as evident when He blesses us with the knowledge that something we said gave hope to another person—and we didn't find out 'til much later.

These are the kinds of blessings *God's Unexpected Blessings* reveals. In it you'll find yourself responding with surprise and hope as you read 52 delightful stories, designed to bless you every week of the year. And after you enjoy a story, you'll meditate on my reflection about the blessing God designed, along with a reflection question to make it personal and meaningful in your own life. After the reflection page, you'll find an additional two pages for you to write down your journaled thoughts and impressions.

Why not use this charming and beautiful book as your daily journal? You'll find a verse to focus your concentration on the Lord, a compelling story to enrich your heart, a reflection and question to stir your mind, and a journaling opportunity to express your soul.

I expect *God's Unexpected Blessings* will be an unexpected blessing in your life.

K<small>ATHY</small> C<small>OLLARD</small> M<small>ILLER</small>

And we know that God causes all things to work together for good to those who love God, to those who are called according to His purpose.

ROMANS 8:28

God's Creative Blessings

Sharon Hanby-Robie

As CREATIVE DIRECTOR for Starburst Publishers, *God's Unexpected Blessings* is especially exciting for me because it is an idea I have been thinking about for over a year. It actually began with a real life experience I had when I was diagnosed with cancer at 28. At the time, I could not imagine how God would use that devastating experience for my good, so I challenged Him. "God, I believe your words but I'm struggling with knowing how any good can come out of something like this. I'll trust You but You've got to show me Your blessing. Show me how this can bring good for someone." At the time, it was a desperate plea for God to comfort me and encourage me. He did more than that.

I sought out six different doctors before I found one who would stand in faith and agreement with me. I know God doesn't heal everyone, but because of many indications of God's will, I had a complete peace that He would heal me. And He did. And then I began to see the blessings God had planned. While working as an interior designer, God allowed me to be a witness to my mostly Jewish clientele. They watched in amazement at this crazy Christian who stood firm in believing Jesus would heal her. Plus, God blessed me with a ministry to others who found themselves in the scary place of dealing with cancer.

Over the next several years, physicians began to refer patients to me. I counseled them to become experts in their own particular cancers, so they could make educated decisions with regard to therapy and treatment. I also prayed, cried, wrote, and comforted them. I encouraged them to express themselves and their fears to me without feeling a need to protect me. Most people in life-threatening situations find it difficult to be really honest with family and loved ones, for fear of making it even more difficult for those they love.

The greatest blessing, however, came in 1987. I had briefly met a couple the night before at a dinner party. On Sunday morning they called because they had just found out that the sixteen-year-old girl that baby-sat their children had been diagnosed with a tumor in her pelvis. Amputation was scheduled for the next morning. They asked me to go to the hospital and speak with her and her parents.

I was a stranger to that family, but God empowered me with the right words. He prepared their hearts to receive my suggestion that they transfer her to Sloan Kettering Memorial Hospital in New York. There she was treated with an experimental heat therapy.

It is now ten years later, and she is a beautiful twenty-six-year-old woman with only a slight limp. God used my experience of cancer, and the knowledge I gained through it, to bless a young woman with the gift of keeping her leg.

That experience taught me that we often don't experience God's blessings because we are focused only on ourselves and our problems of the day. It also changed my life. I have learned to look at life with a "bigger picture" view. God never ceases to amaze me and He is always faithful to His promise of blessing.

❧ *Reflections*

SHARON'S EXPERIENCE helps us to remember that we only see the "small picture" of life, but God sees its totality. Our vision is limited, but His is unrestrained. We stand on the shore of life and concentrate on the sand and the waves rolling toward us. God's view takes in not only our tiny earth, but the whole Universe as well. We cry out, "You can't bless or use this, God." And as simply as we build a sandcastle on that shore, He fashions a blessing far beyond what we could have comprehended. Sometimes our sandcastle dissolves as the waves crash onto it, but God's blessings never dissipate. They are permanent. We just have to expand our vision. Try envisioning the country beyond the ocean view sometime. Our spiritual vision can, by faith, imagine the blessings beyond our limited border.

Is there some way that your vision is staying focused on the sand and God wants you to look out over the ocean? He knows what He's doing, even though it's beyond your ability to see. Trust Him for His blessings.

❧ Journal

_____
_____
_____
_____
_____
_____
_____
_____
_____
_____
_____
_____
_____
_____
_____
_____
_____
_____
_____
_____
_____
_____
_____
_____
_____
_____

❧ Journal

O LORD, you are my God; I will exalt you
and praise your name, for in perfect faithfulness you have done marvelous things, things
planned long ago.

ISAIAH 25:1

Expert Credentials For An Unexpected Ministry

Barbara Johnson

In 1966, my husband, Bill, was critically injured in an automobile accident. I had been following his car up into the mountains when I found him sprawled in the middle of a high, winding, tortuous road, almost dead, and severely brain-damaged. During the time when the doctors didn't think he would live, and then during his recovery, I had to learn to cope with parenting in a new and lonely way. I didn't know at the time that God was developing strength within me for the coming trials, these involving our children.

Then, in 1968, our son Steve was killed in Vietnam. I thought at first that no one could bear such pain and loss and still survive; but the grace and strength of God upheld me, and warm Christian friends provided the shoulders I needed for my tears, and the smiles I needed for recovery. In fact, God soon began using me to help other parents who had experienced the death of a child. God had "peeled" me off the ceiling once, and He was putting me to good use.

I was in the pits again in 1973. Our wonderful son Tim, who had just dedicated his life to Christ during the summer while he was vacationing in Alaska, was killed by a drunken driver in a horrible head-on collision on his way home. My immediate reaction was one of shock and anger: "It's unfair! Why would God take him now, just when he had begun sharing His love with others?" Then, slowly, I began to be aware through the circumstances that God had a plan to reach others through Tim's death—people Tim couldn't have reached if he had been alive.

Of course, I felt great grief and sorrow, but I also could see God's hand in the whole situation. As I stood in the mortuary, waiting to identify Tim's broken body, I was reliving an old, bad dream. This was the very same room, the same wallpaper, the same carpeting, the same everything as it had been when Steve was killed—except there was another box with another boy in it. How unbelievable that this could happen to us twice—just five years to the day.

I saw the shattered body and signed another paper stating that this was the right name to go with the crumpled body of our son. But God reminded me that this was not Tim. This was only his earthly shell. Tim was not there. And I began to see the glory in all this. It was as if I could look up and see Tim standing there, all bright and smiling at me, saying, "Don't cry, Mother. I am here with Jesus. I am finally Home! Don't feel bad." We tried to reflect that attitude at Tim's "Coronation Service." We didn't call it a funeral, because we were celebrating his triumphant homegoing. My sister and I wore green dresses—symbolizing life. We completed the uplifting service with the entire audience joining in the singing of "The Hallelujah Chorus." Tim's death launched us into one of the most exciting ministries I've ever known—helping other hurting parents to begin to live again.

🕊 *Reflections*

Since Barbara wrote those words, God has expanded her ministry in tremendous ways, further reaching out to parents whose children have chosen a wayward life style. Our great God is an economic God who doesn't waste any of our life's experiences. We are entitled to grieve and, in fact, we won't be effective unless we go through that process. Yet after the grieving, God promises to bring us to "morning's joy" through a new purpose in reaching out to others. Thousands are grateful that Barbara has chosen to allow her grief to help others through her "Spatula Ministries." Certainly that's been unexpected for Barbara but not for God.

If you have experienced a deep grief, what unexpected blessings has God brought from it? They may not remove all your grief but they can allow you to smile just a little in the midst of the pain.

Journal

Journal

Sons are a heritage from the Lord, children a reward from him.

PSALM 127:3

God's Surprise Package

Lynn D. Morrissey

After seventeen years of marriage, for my fortieth birthday present, the Lord delivered a surprise package wrapped in pink, a precious baby daughter named Sheridan. She is a treasure I absolutely cherish, but one I initially struggled with receiving.

I never wanted to be a mother; the prospect frightened me to death. I was intimidated by the enormous responsibility of raising a child and by my many inadequacies. I knew nothing about children and couldn't relate to them. I had a morbid fear of dying in childbirth; having a child at forty only exacerbated it.

And even were the pregnancy uncomplicated, I dreaded the long haul, feeling as if I'd be raising a child until I were eighty. How would I have the physical stamina to keep pace with an active toddler and the fortitude to combat twenty-first century evils that would undermine my parenting? The big picture overwhelmed me; I felt trapped.

Well-meaning Christian friends suggested abortion. Yet Psalm 139 proved this child wasn't a cosmic accident, but God's creation, whom He was knitting intricately in utero. I didn't doubt God's will, yet struggled intensely with accepting it. Pressured by friends' advice and my own fear, I considered abortion. Yet, by God's grace, I clung to truth and couldn't uproot what He'd planted.

I wrote about my struggle, frailty, and surrender in my journal: "My body contains a secret seed, immortally conceived, mortally sown. Momentarily, I enfold creation. A fragment of eternity forms concentrically like a pearl. Can I bear weight of priceless cargo? Can a broken vessel store treasure of such worth?

"Can an earthen jar contain a soul outlasting every star? Can I refuse? Can I uproot the hidden seed? Can I coerce the Potter to remold the brittle clay—remake the fragile vessel for some other use?

"I can consent. I can surrender to the engendering Spirit. I can open utterly to His infilling glory. I am willing to unveil the pearl at any price. I will become a chalice for the Maker's grace."

Although I willingly refused to abort, I didn't gracefully surrender motherhood to God. I rebelliously complained, questioning His wisdom and resenting His timing. How could I leave a twenty-year career and financial security when I'd worked so hard to achieve success? Wouldn't I look ridiculous as a forty-year-old "dinosaur" swapping diaper rash remedies with my twenty-year-old counterparts?

Although my emotions vacillated between anger and apathy, I prayed that God would change my heart, endowing me with motherly feelings. I clung to truth, that despite my opinion, this child was a gift and reward.

And then it happened. From the moment I held Sheridan, God miraculously replaced my heart of stone with a mother's heart of tenderness. I wrote in my journal: "Now that I see, touch, and communicate with her, absolutely everything is different!"

Sheridan, herself, is an unexpected blessing, arriving late in my life, despite physical "odds" against conception. Yet this lanky five-year-old, who blossomed from only two microscopic cells, is living testimony of life's miracle, leaving me in awe of God's creation. Because I chose life despite my feelings, God allows me to bless others by encouraging them not to abort.

Sheridan transformed me; she's my mid-life "replacement therapy"—replacing my lethargy with her energy, depression with joy, cynicism with optimism, jadedness with innocence, workaholism with play. I've grown mentally as Sheridan and I explore her world, emotionally as Michael and I draw closer in raising our daughter, and spiritually, totally dependent on God for mothering. Without a full-time career, I devote much more time to God. Now He, alone, is my identity, not my job.

When God brought me home to raise Sheridan, He unexpectedly fulfilled my longtime dream of becoming a writer, which working full-time didn't permit. And Sheridan continues to bless me with many amusing anecdotes about which to write.

Reflections

WHEN WE ACCEPT GOD'S WILL, no matter how frightening or unpleasant it may seem, it becomes a joy and God equips us to fulfill it. Lynn experienced that as God miraculously equipped her for motherhood—unexpectedly. She had to let go of worldly security and identity through her job, and found that Christ could become both for her. When we let go of our own dreams, He replaces it with better ones. He may do it in the most amazing, unexpected way—but He promises it will be a blessing.

Are you holding onto one of your own dreams even though you sense God never gave it to you? Let go and receive His better blessing.

Journal

Journal

"For I know the plans that I have for you,"
declares the Lord, "plans for welfare and not for
calamity to give you a future and a hope."

JEREMIAH 29:11

Every Problem Will Change You

Robert H. Schuller

RECENTLY I WAS TALKING to a supersuccessful salesperson. His income is in the six-figure bracket. When I inquired about his training, I was surprised to learn that his degree is in history and education.

"Dr. Schuller, the truth is that I was a very boring teacher. Because I was boring, my students were restless and I failed to communicate to them. I was a boring teacher because I was a bored teacher. My boredom rubbed off on the students. It was not a good situation. Because I had a problem with students, my contract was not renewed—actually I was fired. When the school fired me I became so angry I decided to go out and make something of myself. I went out and landed a better job."

And then he shared a gem of a line. He looked at me with flashing eyes and said, "I had to get fired before I got fired up!" He went on to explain. "Basically, I was too lethargic. My contract cancellation jolted me out of a lazy rut. I'll always be grateful that I was fired, for it made me angry enough at myself to get up and get going."

Reflections

IT'S ALL IN OUR ATTITUDE whether we see God's
unexpected blessings—especially if we get fired from our job.
Yet the man described by Robert Schuller learned the valuable
lesson that good can come from failure—yes, even failure. Most
of us regard failure as the end of the road but God says it's only
a new fork in the road, a beginning to greater blessings. Can we
open our eyes to see the twist in the pavement and abandon our
tunnel vision? Just as Robert Schuller's friend was relieved of
something that didn't suit him, we may find ourselves in a better
job or situation. It may be revealed through failure.

When has failure been a fork in the road to unexpected
blessings for you? In what way is tunnel vision preventing you from seeing God's new twist in your life?

Journal

✑ Journal

_____

_____

_____

_____

_____

_____

_____

_____

_____

_____

_____

_____

_____

_____

_____

_____

_____

_____

_____

_____

Journal

Because of the LORD's great love we are not consumed, for his compassions never fail. They are new every morning; great is your faithfulness.

LAMENTATIONS 3:22, 23

I Don't Really Want To Hurt My Child

Kathy Collard Miller

Darcy's training pants were wet again. Again!
Marching over to my two-year-old daughter, I directed her into the bathroom. As I struggled to pull down the soaking pants, I felt a rush of frustration and a sense of failure.

"Darcy, you're supposed to come in the bathroom and go in the potty chair. Why can't you learn?" I continued to berate her. As I began spanking her with my hand, my tension found an outlet. Spanking changed to hitting.

Darcy's uncontrollable screaming brought me back to reason. Seeing the red blister on her bottom, I dropped to my knees.

"How can I act this way?" I sobbed. "I love Jesus. I don't really want to hurt my child. Oh God, please help me."

The rest of that day I held my anger in check. The next day started out pleasantly. I watched my happy daughter. "How could I ever be angry with you or want to hurt you?"

But as the day progressed and pressures closed in on me, I became impatient again. As the weeks turned into months, my anger habit worsened. At times I grew so violent that I hit my toddler in the head. Other times I kicked her or slapped her face.

As a Christian for ten years, I was ashamed. *Oh, God,* I prayed over and over again, *please take away my anger.* Yet no matter how much I prayed, I could not control my anger when Darcy didn't perform according to my desires. I wondered whether I might kill Darcy in one of my next rages. In time, I had to be honest with myself—I was abusing her.

I was afraid to tell Larry, my husband. After all, he's a policeman. He's arresting people for the very things I'm doing. *What will my friends think of me? I can't tell them either because I lead a Bible study.*

One day I realized Larry had left his off duty service revolver in the bureau drawer. Convinced God no longer loved me and had given up on me, I concluded suicide was the only answer. Then I wouldn't hurt Darcy any more. Thankfully, God's grace prevented me from killing myself.

Even though suicide was no longer an option, I still didn't have any hope.

Soon after, I shared briefly with a neighbor about my anger. She didn't condemn me like another friend had when I'd tried to share my pain. *Oh, Lord, maybe there's hope for me after all,* I cried out when I left her house that day.

From that point on, God seemed to break through my despair and little by little revealed the underlying causes and the solutions for my anger.

Eventually, I had the courage to share my problem with my Bible study group. James 5:16 admonishes us to *admit your faults to one another and pray for each other so that you may be healed* (NASB). They prayed for me and their prayers indeed had "wonderful results."

Through a difficult process of growth of over a year, God's Holy Spirit empowered me to be the loving, patient mother to Darcy that I wanted to be. I learned many principles during that time that I now share in the parenting books I've written like *When Counting to Ten Isn't Enough.* I also teach parenting seminars and speak nationally and internationally. Whereas I once had no hope, I now share hope with others.

I'm thankful to the Lord for healing the relationship between Darcy and me. A beautiful 23-year-old, Darcy has forgiven me for the way I treated her. We share a close relationship and have written a book together called, *Staying Friends With Your Kids.*

I doubted during that distressing time of my life whether God could use something as horrible as child abuse to help others, but He has. That is truly an expected blessing that demonstrates God's great power and unconditional love. I'm so thankful that He never gives up on us.

❧ Reflections

When I was caught at the bottom of that pit of anger and bitterness, I couldn't even see the edge of the pit. When I thought of Romans 8:28, I concluded it must read, *And we know that God causes all things* (except child abuse) *to work together for good* . . . I certainly didn't imagine that God could bring good out of child abuse, much less unexpected blessings! Yet, that's exactly what He did. The wonderful ministry of speaking and writing that He has given me is far beyond what I could ever have imagined. It's to God's praise and glory that He is powerful enough to use anything that we offer Him. He knows how to bless everything.

In what way are you putting an exception into the truth of Romans 8:28? Renew your faith today that nothing, absolutely nothing, is too powerful to overcome God's ability to bring blessings.

Journal

Journal

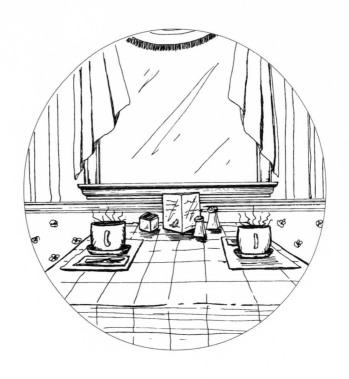

I was pushed back and about to fall,
but the LORD helped me.
The LORD is my strength and song;
he has become my salvation.

PSALM 118:13,14

From Disaster To Blessing

Patricia A.J. Allen

W<small>E SAT IN THE COFFEE SHOP</small> on the town square. The coffee's aroma was as pleasant as Barbara's companionship. The manager interrupted us. "Are you Patricia Allen?" Her smile was guarded. She handed me her cellular phone. "I believe it's your husband."

David's voice quivered when he spoke. Paranoia had him nearly hysterical. "Pat? You've got to come home. I need you. The doctor says you gotta take me to the hospital. I'm scared."

"I'm on my way, honey." My voice was soft, but undergirded with the firmness that would become a primary part of my life style.

David was in the middle of a complete nervous breakdown. He had been so strong in our 30-year marriage. He was a retired Marine. He had served in Vietnam. He was my hero. Yet, he cowered in the car as I drove the forty-five minutes to the psychiatric hospital to which he had been referred. The agony in my heart seemed unbearable as I left him and the heavy doors locked behind me.

Two weeks later, David was released. He came home an old man with shuffling steps; one who had to be encouraged to look at anything beyond his feet. Our finances, relationship, home life, and future were one disaster after another.

I was thankful that his in-hospital and outpatient care were Bible based and administered with firm compassion. Because of his treatment, David had hope. He knew he was hurting, but he believed God's Word about healing and he knew his Lord. Neither of us realized how much work God had to do. In time, he healed David's physical brain of the damage done in the breakdown and Godly therapy healed scars from childhood that had been unknown to either of us. Through it all David's childlike faith seldom wavered.

I went from common housewife to virtual widow to caretaker of a stranger—an adult child—in one day. I also went from believing us to be financially solvent to realizing we were without savings and totally bankrupt. There was no encouragement to believe David could ever work again. I realized that he might need 24 hour a day care for several years. Then came the realization that, with no college or technical training, no recent job experience and a 51-year-old body, I was the sole support of our family

Through a counselor at the state job service, I was invited to join a support group for out-of-work professionals. I had been a custom dressmaker and was a published writer, which qualified me. The group met once a week. David was, by that time, able to be left alone for short periods. Through the group I learned of Sex Equity grants available to individuals wanting to train for specific professions. Even though I had no idea what I wanted or could learn to do, I did know that starting a minimum wage job at my age was not going to pay hospital and retirement expenses. I contacted the administrator at the community college.

As I write this, my husband is mostly healed. He is back to work, albeit at a different job from the managerial position he had held. He is respected at the factory. His work is valued.

I am going to college on a full scholarship and grant, even my travel expenses are being paid. I will be something I never dreamed of becoming—a furniture designer. Had David not broken, I would not have had the courage to find a dream and reach for it. Because God gave us His blessing during the hard times, I have the privilege of developing a career. At a season when many are thinking of retiring, I am beginning. I am not the oldest person on campus, but I am the oldest and most enthusiastic freshman in the furniture lab. I have learned that my God can turn the darkest clouds into the most beautiful of sunsets.

❧ *Reflections*

PATRICIA COULD HAVE GROANED in despair over such seemingly insurmountable difficulties. Yet her faith held firm and in the midst of pain, God's rays of light broke through the dark clouds to create a stunning light show of blessings, something she could not have planned. When you and I begin to doubt in God's ability to bring good out of pain, we can trust His promise that He never gives up on us and will reveal the "way out," even as we grope through the darkness. The joy of the morning's dawn will awaken us to see His hand on everything. Even when we wonder—even if we complain—that He has forsaken us.

How are your difficulties creating doubt in God's ability to strengthen you? Make a fresh commitment to make Him your "strength and song."

Journal

Journal

No temptation has seized you except what is common to man. And God is faithful; he will not let you be tempted beyond what you can bear. But when you are tempted, he will also provide a way out so that you can stand up under it.

I Corinthians 10:13

Unexpected Protection

Charles Swindoll

THE APOSTLE PAUL GIVES US HOPE in this verse of Scripture.

No temptation has overtaken you but such as is common to man; and God is faithful, who will not allow you to be tempted beyond what you are able, but with the temptation will provide the way of escape also, that you may be able to endure it.

A close look at these words reveals something we tend to forget when we're tempted: God is there through it all. He is faithful. We may feel alone, but we are not alone. He places definite limitations on the attack, not allowing the magnet to be stronger than we can bear. And He also promised to provide "the way of escape" so that we aren't totally surrounded and consumed by the temptation. Left completely to ourselves, abandoned, and forgotten by God, we would have no hope of victory. But God is faithful. He doesn't leave us in the lurch. Never.

I once heard a father tell of his son's first serious conflict at school. His boy was being picked on by two or three bullies. They punched the youngster a time or two, pushed him over when he was riding his bike home from school, and generally made life miserable for the lad. They told him they would meet him the next morning and beat him up.

That evening the dad really worked with the boy at home. He showed him how to defend himself, passed along a few helpful techniques, and even gave him some tips on how he might try to win them over as friends. The next morning the lad and dad prayed together, knowing the inevitable was sure to happen. With a reassuring embrace and a firm handshake, the father smiled confidently and said, "You can do it, son. I know you'll make out all right."

Choking back the tears, the boy got on his bike and began the long, lonely ride to school. What the boy did not know was that every block he rode, he was under the watchful eye of his dad . . . who drove his car a safe distance from his son, out of sight but ever ready to speed up and assist if the scene became too threatening. The boy thought he was alone, but he wasn't at all. The father was there all the time.

Reflections

WHEN TEMPTATION LURES US with its attractive
bait, we may think the Lord has abandoned us, just like the little
boy in Charles' story. We may feel alone and unimportant. "Why
doesn't the Lord protect me? Why isn't He here with me? If He
loved me, He would deliver me." We may not be able to see
obvious evidence of His protection and presence, but the Lord
God Almighty is with us. He promises never to leave us or forsake us. He is even more powerful than the human father in our
story. The temptation may seem strong, but look with your spiritual eyes. Our Heavenly Father is there, offering the blessed
help we need. Unexpectedly, in a surprising way, He'll reveal
whatever we need.

Does it seem like Jesus is following from too far to be
of help in your temptation? Claim His promise that
there is a way out. He is closer than you think.

Journal

Journal

Keep your lives free from the love of money and be content with what you have, because God has said, "Never will I leave you; never will I forsake you."

HEBREWS 13:5

Oh, Give Me A Home

Rebecca Thesman

As I CARRIED BOXES into my friend's new house, I wondered if I would ever be so lucky. All my friends and relatives were moving up in the real estate market while I lived in an old two-story house with cracked wallpaper and faded drapes.

Our Sunday School class celebrated each new house with a party, and I cheerfully joined in thanksgiving for my friends' blessings. But I felt alone, the only woman in my peer group whose address had not changed.

So I decided to redecorate my house. I visited craft shows to find the right country accents with ducks and hearts. I ordered a new sofa with blue and mauve checks. Colorful throws and fluffy pillows added a homey touch. I flipped through the pages of decorating magazines, looking for additional ideas that would make my house beautiful.

Two weeks and a small fortune later, I looked around the house and thought, it's still not right. Down came the drapes and the old wallpaper, up went country curtains and borders. I borrowed from our savings account and used my birthday money to buy new accessories and collectibles.

The house soon resembled a magazine cover, but I was not happy with it. Although my home sported popular accents and colors, it was still just an old house. I wanted a new place in a cozy cul-de-sac. Up went the realtor's sign as I began the tour of homes.

I walked through modern castles, three bedroom ranches, and stately colonials. All of them had something I liked, but a stone house on the edge of town had the floor plan I wanted and the location I craved. It was decorated in my colors and had a dream kitchen overlooking the back yard. I imagined my family sitting beside the fireplace, munching popcorn, and sharing Bible verses. My son would sleep peacefully in his color-coordinated bedroom while my husband and I enjoyed the luxury of a master bath. I wanted that house more than anything in the world.

"How much?" I asked the Realtor.

"$82,000."

My dream disappeared in the reality of the housing market. We could never afford a home like that, not on a teacher's salary. My husband would just have to get a better job.

"I don't want to resign," he said. "Besides, I like our house."

The lottery was out of the question. None of my relatives were rich enough to leave me a fortune, and none of them looked like they were ready to keel over. My checks from freelance writing were small and sporadic. No publishers wanted to give me a Michener-sized advance for my book. Besides all that, nobody wanted to buy our old house.

Then I remembered a Bible verse that had been hiding in my tortured consciousness. Moses carried it down the mountain, but it was appropriate for a desperate woman of the nineties. *You shall not covet your neighbor's house* (Exodus 20:17a).

"Whoa, God. I'm not coveting. I'm just tired of my old house."

"You shall not covet your neighbor's house."

"How come I can't have what I want?"

"You shall not covet your neighbor's house."

After three times, the message sunk in. I fell to my knees on the frayed carpet. My discontent had led me to sin, and I was guilty before Almighty God. I had fallen into the trap of adult peer pressure, ignoring the blessing of a debt-free life and a solidly built home. I confessed my covetousness, then looked around the living room.

Some of my decorating changes were good, and my arrangement of furniture was comfortable and stylish. I did not have a four bedroom, two bath house with separate living areas and a jacuzzi in the master suite. I had a roomy two-story that whispered, "Home." My house was a blessing, a gift from my Abba Father, and I needed to thank Him for it every day. As I realized that contentment begins with satisfaction in what I already have, I started thinking about Christ instead of things.

Then my husband and I began to teach the high school Sunday School class. Sunday mornings stretched into Sunday afternoons and extended to Saturday evenings as the kids made our house their headquarters. We popped corn, played Trivial Pursuit, and watched movies. Our old house, spacious enough to accommodate thirty six-foot seniors, became the hang out place in town. Gradually, other kids joined us, then came to Sunday School.

Years later, we watched one of those boys become our church youth pastor. Another couple married and became involved in church music ministries. Another boy was baptized. A painfully shy young man became the sound expert for our worship services. Of course, God performed these miracles, but I like to think my old house contributed. It became a house of unexpected blessings.

Now I know I do not need a fancy house. Christ built me a mansion in heaven. I can hardly wait for the tour.

✺ *Reflections*

REBECCA LEARNED THE BLESSINGS of contentment about the material things of life. How easy it is to be caught up in a love of possessions and money. We've all felt the discontented whisperings of a bigger home, new car, and fashionable clothing. We easily fall prey to society's mantra that "the grass looks greener on the other side of the fence." Yet someone has also pointed out that, "if the grass looks greener on the other side of the fence, just remember their water bill is higher." We will be showered with unexpected blessings as we remember that happiness is something that happens to us, but contentment is something we choose. When the green-eyed monster of envy stares us down, let's defend ourselves with the knowledge that God will provide for our true needs. And in His generosity He frequently gives us our wants, too.

What is stealing your joy and contentment? You may think getting your wish list fulfilled will bring blessings, but contentment in itself is a complete unexpected blessing. Seek it this week.

✍ Journal

✍ Journal

_____

_____

_____

_____

_____

_____

_____

_____

_____

_____

_____

_____

_____

_____

_____

_____

_____

_____

_____

Journal

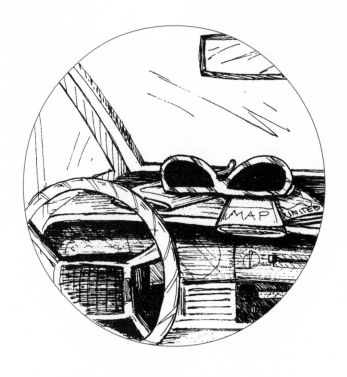

And God is able to make all grace abound to
you, so that in all things at all times, having
all that you need, you will abound in every
good work.

II CORINTHIANS 9:8

Unexpected Blessing In Marriage

Ellen Bergh

MOST PEOPLE CHART A COURSE for a driving vacation with detailed maps, planned rest stops, and orderly travel. We are not those people. We'd been married fifteen years before we embarked on a vacation on the road. We planned to just go with the flow.

The itinerary looked like a no-brainer. Los Angeles to Yosemite to Portland Oregon and return. What could go wrong? At Yosemite, we rafted in the green waters of the Merced and savored the forest glade. The discord developed as we packed our Datsun truck for the next leg of the trip.

I'm a morning person, a revved up rabbit type raring to be on the road at first light. My husband, the turtle type, slowly stowed the camping equipment with such precision you'd have thought he expected border inspection by the Perfection Patrol. I stood by mentally drumming my fingers. Finally, we left Yosemite at 10:30 a.m. putting us on Interstate 5 through central California during the 100 degree day. As a hot wind blew through the tiny truck, I came to a slow boil, replaying in my mind how this all could have been avoided, if only he'd listened to me. I told him we needed to get going earlier.

The eternal day ended after a two hour tie-up in traffic. We wearily pulled into Stockton in early evening and pried ourselves off the hot seats. I flounced into the motel room, sulking over the ordeal we'd been through. While the rest of the family frolicked in the pool, I lay on the bed projecting what horrors lay ahead tomorrow if we got another slow start.

Later that evening, noticing my glum mood, my husband asked, "What would it take to make you happy?"

"I'd be happy if we don't dawdle along like today. We need to be on the road before dawn so we can avoid this heat. Then, I'd feel we were making some progress."

But my victory seemed hollow at 5:00 a.m. next morning, when we trooped out to the truck. Our lanky daughter refused to ride up front with the feuding folks, preferring to perch on top of the camping gear. We pulled onto Interstate 5, the euphoria of yesterday in Yosemite a hazy memory. We rode along in strained silence.

Ten miles out of Stockton, a car sat stranded beside the freeway in the predawn. I cringed. My husband traces his lineage back to the Good Samaritan. Surely, he won't think of stopping. He knows we need to press on to get out of the hot central valley.

But as we passed the car, we saw a man, woman, and three little girls in frilly party dresses shivering in the back seat. My husband looked over at me, and I reluctantly nodded. He pulled over onto the shoulder and backed up to the disabled vehicle.

While the men set to work with his tools, my daughter and I dispensed old sweatshirts, donuts, and fruit juice to the woman and her daughters.

She explained, "We'd been to a family reunion in Stockton and got a late start home. The car died and we watched people whiz by without stopping all night long. The girls cried themselves to sleep."

My heart broke, thinking of their fear and discomfort.

While our daughter stayed with the girls, the woman and I settled in our truck. We exchanged stories of how both of us had read the riot act to our men the night before. We shook our heads and hoped to do better.

Their car fixed, we caravaned to their turnoff in Sacramento. Waving them a good-bye, my husband met my gaze. We burst out laughing. We both knew whose unexpected timetable we were really on. I shoved my map under the seat and scooted over closer. In helping someone else, God had healed my road rage and brought blessings in our journey.

❧ Reflections

ELLEN EXPERIENCED TWO VALUABLE LESSONS on that trip: one which was a great blessing to others and another one that strengthened her marriage. We can miss great blessings in our marriage and friendships when we want something done our way, and we're certain it's the only right way. Yet, Ellen learned, "different isn't necessarily wrong" about her and her husband's different inner time clocks. So much of the success of marriage is wrapped in seeing life from our spouse's perspective. If we'll put on their "frame of reference," we may see something valuable: like God's unexpected blessings.

How does your spouse bother you at times? If you adjust your perspective, could you see a blessing in it instead?

❧ Journal

Journal

. . . whatever you did for one of the least of
these brothers of mine, you did for me.

MATTHEW 25:40

Waiting For The 12:35

Doris C. Crandall

CHRIS DOWELL HAD FINISHED a long weekend of intensive training for volunteering at a crisis hot line for students at Oklahoma University. It is called Number Nyne, and when students feel angry, upset, frustrated, depressed or lonely, they can call and talk to the volunteers. He was going home from work at about 10:00 p.m. the day after he'd finished the course.

Going over some railroad tracks, Chris saw a wheelchair out of the corner of his eye. He drove on to the stop sign on the other side of the tracks thinking, "I wonder what that guy is doing there? He's sitting way too close to be waiting to cross the tracks. Oh, well, it's not my problem."

Suddenly something inside him made Chris change his mind. Putting the truck into reverse, he backed up to the man in the wheelchair. Rolling down the passenger side window, Chris called out, "Hey, what's going on? Do you need any help?"

The man didn't answer, so Chris parked, walked over to him and sat on the ground next to his wheelchair. "I'm just waiting," the man mumbled.

"What for?"

"A train. Old Jess is going to kiss this world good-bye. Man, I'm paralyzed. I can't walk and can't hardly use my arms."

"You sound really down. What has gotten you so upset?" Chris didn't try to talk him out of his plans or push him off the track. He knew the next train wouldn't come until 12:35. He just listened as he told him his troubles. They talked about two hours.

Finally, Jess said he'd changed his mind. "Chris, man," he said, "I don't know if you believe in God, but I do. Before I came to these tracks tonight I prayed, 'Look, God, I'm going to the railroad tracks and kiss the first train that comes by. I don't know if that's what You want but if it's not, then send somebody to stop me,' and He did. He sent you."

Chris was astounded. He could see how God had prepared him to respond to Jess. That summer he had experienced three specific instances where he knew God was taking care of him. The Lord had also prepared him through the course he had just taken dealing with suicidal people. He knew all this was no mere coincidence.

This unexpected blessing made Chris' heart soar with happiness. Somehow he and Jess got to laughing and rejoicing. Soon they heard the whistle of the 12:35. Chris pushed Jess' chair back and they hugged each other as they watched the train rumble down the track.

God had done something for someone else using Chris as a tool. "I thank God that I listened when that voice inside my heart said, 'Back up and talk to that man.'"

❦ *Reflections*

IF CHRIS HADN'T RESPONDED to God's prompting, a man's life would have been snuffed out. Doris' story reminds us of the importance of promptly obeying the Lord. He will prepare us for anything He wants to do with us. And if we don't feel capable, He will empower us in the moment we need it. Chris relied upon that truth when he was faced with an unexpected challenge and blessing. It resulted in an unspeakable joy as God used him. You and I can experience the same thrill as lives are impacted through our obedience. If we'll respond to God's challenge, we'll experience similar blessings.

What challenge are you facing? Why do you hesitate responding? If God is calling you, He'll empower you. Step out in faith.

Journal

❧ Journal

_____

_____

_____

_____

_____

_____

_____

_____

_____

_____

_____

_____

_____

_____

_____

_____

_____

_____

_____

_____

_____

_____

. . . *when her baby is born she forgets the anguish because of her joy that a child is born into the world.*

JOHN 16:21b

Next To My Heart

Bonnie Compton Hanson

T HE DAY I HAD TO STOP dead in my tracks in the aisle of a busy supermarket was one of the worst in my whole life.

There I was, pregnant as could be, forty pounds overweight, a whole month past my due date, with wretched "morning sickness" that lasted 24 hours every single day. And now I had charley horses in both feet—so excruciating I couldn't move.

This wasn't the way I had expected motherhood to be. My own mother, who had six children, glowed when she was expecting. Her mother not only joyfully welcomed sixteen little ones into the world, but ran a busy store the whole time. "Looking forward to holding a little one in one's arms," they said, "and feeling the miracle of life inside one, should make any woman ecstatically happy. And healthy!" Why wasn't I experiencing that?

In all my magazines, the maternity advertisements showed blissful mothers-to-be in adorable outfits, perfect hairdos—even high heels. And that's the way my expecting friends were. An office-mate with the same due date as me worked right up till her baby came. My next-door neighbor had done everything she wanted for nine full months while looking absolutely gorgeous. Neither had been ill a minute. And both of them now had adorable, healthy babies.

Meanwhile, I was still pregnant, still miserable, and so large I had long since forgotten what either my feet or my legs looked like. There was only one outfit I could even get on—a sort of muumuu tent. I'd had to give up work, give up church ministries, almost give up hope.

Why was God allowing this to happen to me? He knew I loved Him, my husband, and this unborn child. My friends had started snickering: "You were due when?" Even my doctor grumped at me as if it were all my own fault.

And now during one of the hottest Augusts on record, my ankles swelled so badly in our sweltering apartment, I had to keep them in buckets of ice. Going anywhere was torture. But we were out of milk. Just a quick dash to the store, I thought—surely I could do that.

So here I was, frozen in my tracks, stopping carts in both directions.

My face beet red, I stared at the rows of cracker boxes in front of me—pretending not to notice the angry shoppers whose way I was blocking. And then I heard a little girl's voice: "Mommy, why does that lady look so funny?"

I squeezed my eyes shut, trying to stop sudden tears. *Oh, God, please. That's the last straw. Can't anyone say anything nice about me for a change? I'm so tired of being a medical freak. Won't I ever be normal and comfortable and well again? Won't I ever get to hold this baby in my arms?*

Then that mother said something I will never forget. "Dear," she murmured, "it's because God has given that woman a tiny baby to carry next to her heart."

When I opened my eyes, mother and daughter were gone. In a few minutes, so were the charley horses. But those words have lasted a lifetime.

For, oh, they were so true. They were such a unexpected blessing to me during those final miserable days before I did hold my beautiful firstborn in my arms. During my next two pregnancies, those precious words strengthened me again. It's been a blessing I have been privileged to share with my own pregnant daughters-in-law and many other young women I have known over the years.

For even after our children are born, all mothers still carry those precious little ones next to our hearts—even when they are grown up and have children of their own.

And our dear Heavenly Father carries us next to His. Always. And there's no place I'd rather be.

❦ Reflections

Oh, the power of words. The power of a cutting remark or a strengthening comment. For good or bad. Positive or negative. Bonnie experienced the power of words on that sweltering August day when she had given up hope. Yet, the few words of a compassionate woman have unexpectedly blessed several generations—and that woman isn't even aware of the blessing she birthed. We each need to guard our words, for everything we say will bless or dishearten, bring joy or sorrow, pain or comfort. Bonnie has never forgotten that day when a stranger gave her words of hope. What will we find our words did on this earth when we talk with people in heaven? Let's make them count for an unexpected blessing.

In what ways do you find harmful words springing from your mouth without intending to hurt others? Make a new commitment to guard your tongue and thinking.

Journal

Journal

For God so loved the world that he gave his
one and only Son, that whoever believes in
him shall not perish but have eternal life.

JOHN 3:16

Unexpected Sacrifice

Max Lucado

I T'S DIFFICULT TO FIND BEAUTY IN DEATH. It's even more difficult to find beauty in a death camp. Especially Auschwitz. Four million Jews died there in World War II. A half-ton of human hair is still preserved. The showers that sprayed poison gas still stand.

But for all the ugly memories of Auschwitz there is one of beauty. It's the memory Gajowniczek has of Maximilian Kolbe.

In February, 1941, Kolbe was incarcerated at Auschwitz. He was a Franciscan priest. In the harshness of the slaughterhouse he maintained the gentleness of Christ. He shared his food. He gave up his bunk. He prayed for his captors. He was soon given the nickname "Saint of Auschwitz."

In July of that same year there was an escape from the prison. It was the custom at Auschwitz to kill ten prisoners for every one who escaped. All the prisoners would be gathered in the court-yard and the commandant would randomly select ten names from the roll book. These victims would be immediately taken to a cell where they would receive no food or water until they died.

The commandant begins calling the names. At each selection another prisoner steps forward to fill the sinister quota. The tenth name he calls is Gajowniczek.

As the SS officers check the numbers of the condemned, one of the condemned begins to sob. "My wife and my children," he weeps.

The officers turn as they hear movement among the prisoners. The guards raise their rifles. The dogs tense, anticipating a command to attack. A prisoner has left his row and is pushing his way to the front.

It is Kolbe. No fear on his face. No hesitancy in his step. The capo shouts at him to stop or be shot. "I want to talk to the commander," he says calmly. For some reason the officer doesn't club or kill him. Kolbe stops a few paces from the commandant, removes his hat and looks the German officer in the eye.

"Herr Kommandant, I wish to make a request, please."

That no one shot him is a miracle.

"I want to die in the place of this prisoner." He points at the sobbing Gajowniczek. The audacious request is presented without stammer.

"I have no wife and children. Besides, I am old and not good for anything. He's in better condition." Kolbe knew well the Nazi mentality.

"Who are you?" the officer asks.

"A Catholic priest."

The block is stunned. The commandant, uncharacteristically speechless. After a moment, he barks, "Request granted."

Prisoners were never allowed to speak. Gajowniczek says, "I could only thank him with my eyes. I was stunned and could hardly grasp what was going on. The immensity of it: I, the condemned, am to live and someone else willingly and voluntarily offers his life for me—a stranger. Is this some dream?"

The Saint of Auschwitz outlived the other nine. In fact, he didn't die of thirst or starvation. He died only after the camp doctor injected phenol into his heart. It was August 14, 1941.

Gajowniczek survived the Holocaust. He made his way back to his hometown. Every year, however, he goes back to Auschwitz. Every August 14 he goes back to say thank you to the man who died in his place.

In his backyard there is a plaque. A plaque he carved with his own hands. A tribute to Maximilian Kolbe—the man who died so he could live.[1]

1. This story is adapted from the book *A Man for Others* by Patricia Treece.

🦢 *Reflections*

WE CAN'T IMAGINE the great strength and sacrifice of Maximilian Kolbe as described in Max's story. How did he find the courage to ask for death? What kind of love is this that would offer his own life for a stranger? What an unexpected blessing Gajowniczek experienced.

Yet you and I have received that same kind of unexpected blessing. God's Son Jesus died for us. He was motivated by a great love. He sacrificed Himself even though He knew we weren't worthy of it. Even though He knew we could reject His offer of grace. He still gave His life—and He would have if only one person on earth ever lived—YOU. You were important enough for Him to make that great sacrifice. Both you and Gajowniczek have received the wonderful news of such an unexpected blessing. You don't deserve it, yet the blessing is yours.

How can you make a small sacrifice in love for someone today? It may be something as simple as taking a meal to a sick friend or as deep as choosing to love someone unlovely. Can you do anything else considering the great sacrifice made for you?

Journal

Journal

The blessing of the LORD brings wealth,
and he adds no trouble to it.

PROVERBS 10:22

 *Special Legacy*

Nancy L. Goodwin

It WAS THE DAY AFTER my mother's funeral, following her long illness. I had gone to her apartment to pack up her few belongings. Full of grief, and questioning God's wisdom in taking my dear mom, I sank wearily onto an old kitchen chair to sort through some papers.

"Why my godly mother, Lord? Why such a short and difficult life? What will I do without her wisdom and warm love?"

Her earthly poverty surrounded me, plain evidence of her struggles. As my eyes roamed the sparsely furnished kitchen and the ancient cookstove, my heart broke. I put my head down, weeping, but found a small stack of books in my way. It was Mom's well-worn Bible and several favorite devotional books. I shoved them aside but saw a sheet of notebook paper stuck in one of them. I pulled it out and began to read the lines scrawled on it in a shaky but familiar hand:

Therefore, my dear friends, as you have always obeyed—not only in my presence but now much more in my absence—continue to work out your salvation with fear and trembling, for it is God who works in you to will and act according to his good purpose (Philippians 2:12, 13).

The verses were repeated several times and I realized that it was mom's "memory work." All her life she had memorized God's word. Her very last day at home and only a few days before her death, she had continued to do so. What a special legacy and tender blessing to a sorrowing, searching daughter.

Mom had not known those would be her last memorized verses but our heavenly Father knew. Knowing all things, He lovingly planned a rich and comforting blessing for me as I faced the loss of my mother. Those verses answered my questioning heart in a totally unexpected way, designed by God.

I folded up the cheap note sheet with its priceless words and tucked it safely away as the peace and healing love of God's provision and direction eased my sore spirit. My mother's earthly life was over but her example as a woman of the Book became my bright signpost in a dark place.

I was to "continue working out my salvation," walking on with the Lord my mom introduced me to so long ago. I would be enabled to do His good will by His own presence in me.

I never read those verses without the soft echo of her voice resounding in my heart—my special legacy.

❧ *Reflections*

WE NEVER KNOW HOW THE LORD will meet us in our hurt. He can creatively make a slip of paper with some meaningful words gladden our hearts, just as Nancy experienced. Her mother's faithfulness in valuing the Word of God paid unexpected dividends, even after she left this earth. God knew Nancy's mother would be enjoying His presence soon and planned for Nancy to have the encouragement she would need. Isn't that just like the Lord to arrange something unexpectedly even before it's necessary?

Has the Lord tried to gladden your heart, but since He didn't do it in the way you expected, you haven't acknowledged it? Receive His creative design. He doesn't want you to be discouraged—but encouraged. You are loved.

Journal

❧ Journal

_____
_____
_____
_____
_____
_____
_____
_____
_____
_____
_____
_____
_____
_____
_____
_____
_____
_____
_____
_____
_____
_____

Yet the LORD longs to be gracious to you;
he rises to show you compassion. For the
LORD is a God of justice. Blessed are all
who wait for him!

ISAIAH 30:18

If Heartbeats Could Talk

Lille Diane

THE GUARD WALKED SILENTLY behind me down the corridor to the room holding a piece of my future inside. If heartbeats could talk, mine would have been pleading for my life. I was going to meet prospective foster parents and I feared if I got what I deserved, these people would be worse than my darkest nightmare—and I deserved it.

My mind went wild with thoughts of what the couple would be like. I knew they had read the arrest reports about me and the multiple recommendations by psychologists and probation officers to lock me up for five years until I was twenty-one. Instead, the judge was giving me one chance in a foster home. Whoever waited for me behind the steel door knew they were my only chance out. All I could think was, "Why do they want me?"

The door opened to expose a mystery. The gruesome twosome I'd expected turned out to look more like Ward and June Cleaver with smiles brighter than high beams. I turned back to look at the guard fully expecting to see Rod Sterling telling me I had just entered the Twilight Zone.

Life had taught me when to look cold as ice or sweet as pie-depending on the circumstances. These two people unsettled me, not in a negative way, but in a way that had me wondering who was in control. I knew they had read the facts about me: drugs, runaway, incorrigibility, promiscuity, sexual abuse . . . the list went on and on. I took my seat somehow knowing this was much bigger than me.

After they introduced themselves, they began talking about

their family with joy and pride. I watched in awe. I had been raised by parental figures who gave me the impression I was a mistake. All children were.

Next they discussed their church and their beliefs. I didn't allow my face to show that I was devouring every word as if I were starving for it. But I didn't know how to handle those feelings so I avoided eye contact to hide my interest.

"I understand you like to sing and play the guitar," the woman said softly and sincerely.

On the inside I sat up straight. "Yeah," I said, trying to act indifferent. I waited for the catch.

"That's great!" she said, lighting up the whole room. "We have a singing youth group and band called "Faith Unlimited" that plays all over Southern California. Perhaps if you came to live with us you could join the group."

I shrugged my shoulders, "Yeah, maybe." If heartbeats could talk, mine would have been singing.

"Would you like to come home with us next Saturday to meet the rest of the family?" the man asked.

"Okay. I guess so." Change was in the air. My heart quivered.

Walking back to my cell, I smiled and began making plans of what I would wear to meet the family. I knew I was going home.

The months and years ahead became God's grooming ground for me. Through the love of my foster family, I came to know Jesus as my personal Savior. He used them to encourage me to develop the gifts He had placed inside of me. My foster mother, Fran, spent countless hours with me helping to overcome the hurts, pain, and poor choices I'd made to hide my broken spirit and tattered childhood. She is still my best friend, my spiritual mother.

Today I am a successful speaker, songwriter, recording artist, author, actress, and mural artist. It seems that every day God unfolds more and more treasure buried inside me. Now I am a mentor and role model to those who wonder where their future lies or whether they even deserve one. I can hear their hearts beat.

How could I have known that God would give me such an unexpected blessing when I made the decision to trust that family? If heartbeats could talk, mine would be singing.

❧ Reflections

LILLE'S STORY IS A POWERFUL ONE of God's grace and the unconditional love of a foster family. Her view of herself, because of a traumatic childhood, was damaged and warped. Yet God's view of her was a kaleidoscope of love, grace, power, and joy. He communicated that through the caring of a foster family who looked beyond the hard facade caused by fear and pain.

God can empower us to look beyond a person's protective exterior to see their value within. There may be people who you believe can't possibly be a blessing in your life. Lille's foster family may have wondered whether she would be a blessing, but their faith and love broke through to give birth to a servant of God.

Is there someone in your life that seems beyond reach? Can you trust God enough to reach out to them anyway? You may find a soft interior which will become an unexpected blessing.

Journal

Journal

As iron sharpens iron, so one man sharpens another.

PROVERBS 27:17

The Tortoise And The Hare— Revisited

Kitty Bucholtz

W HEN I DECIDED ON A HUSBAND, I prayed a lot to be sure I was choosing the right man. My heart said I was, but my mind wasn't always so sure. When we were married at the ripe old age of 22, I was smart enough to know this was going to be one of the longest, hardest jobs of my life. Having just spent the last two-and-a-half years getting to know John, I knew "compromise" was going to be the name of the game.

I had it all planned out. First, no changing each other. We knew a lot of people who strived to change their spouse after they married. Most of those couples were struggling. So I decided that if John likes creamy peanut butter—ugh—we would simply buy a jar for him and a jar of crunchy for me. No forcing him to eat crunchy. (I would never give in to eating creamy.)

John insisted on buying Levi's® 501 button fly jeans. After we concluded my "discussion" on the merits of other brands, I finally told him he had a certain number of dollars to spend. He could buy two pairs of Levi's® or four pairs of the other brand. I smugly figured that would be the end of that.

John isn't like me. He bought two pairs of Levi's®.

Last month, after buying two different kinds of toothpaste, I looked at his tube and saw—egad—John squeezes from the middle. Everyone knows, for best results, you squeeze from the end. Every now and then I squeeze it all back to the top for him.

I remember thinking before I got married, "This is going to be hard, but I think I can be as happy with John as I'm going to get. And more importantly, God seems to be saying he's the one. I'll just learn to ignore the irritating things he does like play video games into the wee hours of the morning. I will be patient and pray a lot."

God must have been laughing on His throne. Nothing is like I expected it to be. Over the last eight years, John has grown, matured, and put my holier-than-thou attitude to shame. He cleans the bathrooms, does all the laundry so I can write, cooks most of the meals, rubs my shoulders and feet often without me asking, and spoils me like crazy. Talk about unexpected blessings.

I feel like the tortoise and the hare. When we first got married, I thought I was so wonderful and John needed so much help to be a good husband. Now I am racing to catch up, trying to think of nice little things to do for him like he does for me.

Oh, he's still like a lot of husbands. I still pay all the bills, budget the money, make the appointments, schedule service on the cars, keep track of receipts and rebates and warranties, and schedule our life out to the nth degree. But he keeps me sane with his "Why worry? God will take care of it" attitude.

A little older and a little wiser, I now have one eye on God and one on John, waiting to see who will surprise me next. I know what the Psalmist meant now when he said "my cup runneth over." He meant that when God gives you one big blessing, it's often just the vessel through which a million other blessings will come to you.

❧ Reflections

KITTY WISELY DIDN'T BUY INTO an early marriage foible that many of us unconsciously carry into our relationships: "I'll get him to the altar, and then I'll alter him." Oh, she still had challenges but at least that wasn't one of them! How wonderful that she has wisely seen the hidden blessings of changing her attitude to focus on the positives in John. She prudently acknowledged her wrong ideas of John's need to be "helped" as a husband. Marriage requires a lot of shaping and changing in both the wife's and husband's attitudes. Kitty reveals the unexpected blessings of being "others-centered" rather than "self-centered."

❧

How would the Lord like you to be more "others-centered" in your marriage? Are you still trying to change your spouse? It won't work. Look for the unexpected blessings of concentrating on your mate's good points.

❧ Journal

Journal

And even the very hairs of your head are all
numbered. So don't be afraid; you are worth
more than many sparrows.

MATTHEW 10:30, 31

Not My Breast

Marie Asner

IN THE FALL OF 1994, I was shocked when the mammogram technician said the radiologist needed another view. "This has never happened to me before," I anxiously thought, "it must be a machine malfunction."

After a tense wait, she returned and inquired, "Do you have a surgeon?"

"Surgeon?" I couldn't believe my ears. "No."

A few moments later, the radiologist explained, "I see something that looks like a microcalcification and a biopsy is needed. The dots are star-shaped instead of rounded, which is a questionable sign."

The technician gave me a listing of surgeons and I left the hospital with feelings of dread. "Why me?" I wanted to shout. A small voice inside said, "Why not you." What makes YOU so special?" I ignored the taunting voice and remembered God said that even the hairs on my head were numbered. I remained calm and after arriving home spoke to my husband who reassured me.

Then I began phoning surgeons for consultations. God was indeed with me as I found one who was caring and took time to answer my questions. We set the date for surgery. I placed myself in God's hands, fearing the worst, yet hoping I would fall into "the 80% negative biopsies."

On the day of surgery, I was able to joke with the technician and radiologist who had to place a needle in my breast so the surgeon could locate the exact area. I resisted feeling like a fatality and knew God was with me, ". . . counting the hairs on my head."

I later rejoiced when the biopsy was negative. The calcifications were removed and I healed in record time with only a faint scar. Still, the experience left me shaken and I wondered how best to express my feelings. A friend suggested I write about it, so I did. I wrote an article about my experience, hoping to help other women ease their anxiety about this procedure. It was published in a magazine that, unknown to me, was sent to my hospital.

Months later, when I went for a follow-up exam, several hospital staff recognized me as ". . . the woman who wrote that article." They told me, "Your article is now required reading for personnel here and the magazine is available for patients."

The technician said, "Your experience is now a blessing for our anxious patients."

I never anticipated that God would use my story in that way. It's been a blessing to share with others that God cares about us and "counts even our hairs."

Reflections

THE POSSIBILITY OF CANCER has to be one of the most fearful things any of us could face. Marie encountered that possibility by claiming God's promise that He is intimately acquainted with everything about her. Such a truth can strengthen us in harrowing times. No, that doesn't guarantee the biopsy will always be negative, but it does assure us that God knows exactly what He's doing in our lives. He wants only the best for us and will use everything for good if we'll cooperate.

Marie never could have imagined the blessing of becoming "the woman who wrote that article," but God knew all along His plans to bring good out of it.

Are you facing cancer or some other difficulty, large or small? Or does it seem like life is just too good— something bad must be coming soon? God's guarantee of unanticipated blessings is there for you. Your hairs are numbered.

Journal

✒ *Journal*

*Therefore, I urge you, brothers, in view of
God's mercy, to offer your bodies as living
sacrifices, holy and pleasing to God—this is
your spiritual act of worship.*

ROMANS 12:1

The Unexpected Blessings Of Sacrifice

Billy Graham

In the covered wagon days when the Old West was bulging with gold, the pioneers endured the sufferings of the prairies, the mountains, and the desert, and the savage attacks of the Indians because they knew that beyond those Sierras lay the rewards of golden California.

When Bill Borden, son of the wealthy Bordens, went out to China as a missionary, many of his friends thought he was foolish to "waste his life," as they put it, trying to convert a few heathens to Christianity. But Bill loved Christ and he loved men. He hadn't been out there very long before he contracted an oriental disease and died. At his bedside they found a note that he had written while he was dying. It read: "No reserve, no retreat, and no regrets."

Bill had found more happiness in his few years of sacrificial service than most people find in a lifetime.

❧ Reflections

MOST OF US WANT TO AVOID SACRIFICE. It doesn't have a good reputation. It represents pain, discomfort, and self-lessness. The world system certainly doesn't recommend it. Instead, "Do Your Own Thing" is the proposed philosophy that purportedly brings joy and happiness. Yet, God's heavenly perspective is quite the opposite. He wants us to have an eternal mind-set that sees the secret blessings of sacrifice. Through it we experience God's love and approval and we receive the thanks of others as we serve them. We'll also grow spiritually, enabled to handle life's stresses and strains with more grace and strength. That's true happiness. God's unexpected blessing of joy comes wrapped in the package of sacrifice.

How could you open your package of sacrifice even today? It could mean loving someone who is seemingly unlovely or writing that thank you note that you've been putting off. Or it could be something as complicated as surrendering to God's plan to be a missionary. Unwrap your package. You'll find the gift of unexpected blessings.

Journal

Journal

Journal

Love . . . keeps no record of wrongs.

I CORINTHIANS 13:4, 5

A Very Special Birthday Card

Delores E. Bius

THIS WAS THE FOURTH CARD SHOP I had visited in a futile effort to find just the right card for my father's birthday. I could not honestly choose one of the beautiful ones that proclaimed, "You were always there for me." Rather I needed one that admitted, "You were never there for me." Other years I had picked out a generic "For my Father" card that was rather nondescript.

This year my search was fruitless. Finally I decided, "Oh, just this once I will send him a really special one even if I don't want to!" I picked out a beautiful, expensive card that said, "You were always there for me when I needed you."

Before mailing it, I had a long talk with the Lord. "Lord, I know Your Word tells me that I shouldn't let bitterness dwell in my heart. I forgave my father years ago, but I haven't forgotten all his injustices to me. And he has never acknowledged them. They seem to lurk in my subconscious like a pit of vipers that frequently comes out to nip at me. But since Hebrews 12:15 warns me to make sure bitterness doesn't spring up and trouble me, I'll choose to send him this card, even though he doesn't deserve it."

When he received the card, my Dad telephoned me long distance and admitted, "I've been sitting here looking at this beautiful card you sent me and I must confess that the words in it do not really apply to me. I neglected you all your life."

Hardly able to believe my ears, I reassured him, "Dad, don't you worry about that. You did the best you could. You did lead me to the Lord when I was a teen and my Heavenly Father has always been there for both of us. He forgave my sins and yours and we shall one day see Him in Heaven."

Upon uttering those words, I could feel those vipers inside my soul slither back to the pit of hell where they belonged. The Lord gave me the blessing of true forgiveness toward my father that I had been unable to muster in my own strength.

Only two weeks later, I was standing in the funeral home by my father's casket, amazed at the long procession of mourners who offered me their condolences. Many had tears in their eyes and were obviously deeply moved at the sudden passing of my father.

Someone once said, "Forgiveness is not a case of holy amnesia that wipes out the past. Instead it is the experience of healing that drains the poison from the wound" (source unknown).

How grateful I am that God led me to send my father that very special birthday card. It was a blessing to both of us.

᭭ Reflections

FORGIVING IS HARD. We incorrectly think that forgiving means we're saying what they did was all right. We don't want them to go unpunished for the hurt and pain they caused us. But Delores has offered us the truth that forgiveness brings unexpected blessings in us and the person who hurt us. Forgiving is like peeling an onion. Just when you think you're done forgiving, God reveals another layer that needs to be pulled off. We may resist, but we'll find the hidden blessings in the inside layer of that onion peel.

Is there someone who remains unforgiven in your life? You may think it's hurting them, but it's actually only preventing you from experiencing God's blessings. Forgive them, layer by layer. The blessings will be much sweeter than the smell of that onion.

Journal

Journal

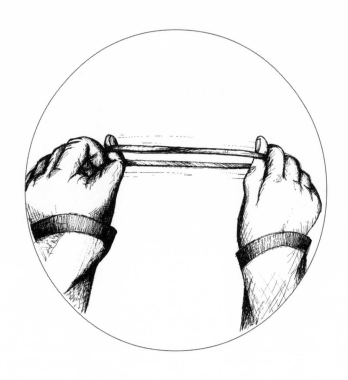

For God did not give us a spirit of timidity, but a spirit of power, of love and of self-discipline.

II Timothy 1:7

Unexpected Emotions

Patsy Clairmont

Sometimes I feel as though my emotions are a tangled wad.

I guess that's why one night, while I was in bed praying for a creative way to visualize emotions, I thought of knotting rubber bands together. I jumped up and found a bag of 100 red, blue, green, and yellow rubber bands. Then I climbed back in bed and began to tie them in a long, snarled chain (probably the closest I've ever come to knitting or crocheting).

My husband came into the room and saw me busy at my stretchy task. He shook his head and muttered, "I knew one day it would come to this."

I often ask my audiences if they brought their emotions with them to the retreat. Usually they giggle, and a number of women raise their hands, signifying they did. Then I ask how many of the gals brought their hormones, and the rest of the hands go up.

When I next pull my emotions out of a bag in the form of my rubber chain, the women titter and nod their recognition. I demonstrate, by tugging at the bands until they appear they will snap, how people sometimes get on my nerves. As I pile the long, variegated snarl into a five-inch-tall heap on my hand, I show them what happens when I don't stay current with my emotions—they become so entangled that I can't tell what I'm feeling. And when I can't identify what I'm feeling, I can't resolve it, which means the knotted mess is growing inside me.

I remember coming home one evening after being with a group of friends and telling Les how angry I was with one of them.

"Really, what did she do?" he inquired.

Well, I told him in no uncertain terms what she did.

When I finished, he said, "I don't think you're angry."

"You don't?" I asked.

"No," he reinforced.

"I feel angry," I assured him.

"I think you're jealous," he stated boldly.

"Jealous?" I screeched.

"Jealous?" I hissed.

Then I slunk into another room to file my nails in private. Alone, I finally asked the Lord if what Les suggested could possibly be true. Immediately I realized he had caught the cat by her claws.

I've been able to work through my jealous feelings in regard to this friend thanks to Les' confrontation. Otherwise, I'd still be rationalizing my anger and not facing the real issue.

When issues aren't faced, they build inside us, which means somebody's going to experience emotional whiplash when we get crossed. The way buildups become blowups is that one day a family member, coworker, friend, or total stranger makes one teeny-tiny comment, and we let that person have it with our entire rubber-band arsenal. He or she doesn't know what happened.

When the person asks, "What's wrong with you?" we shout, "Everything!" shaking all our tangled emotions in his or her face.

Have you ever noticed how quiet a room gets when you over-react? All eyes are on you. Even though no one says it, you know they're wondering what your problem is. But then, so are you, because more often than not, the time and place where you explode are side issues.

I once had a disagreement with a coworker, and when I came home, I started nit-picking on my teenager Jason. I hit him with a lengthy list of criticisms. Baffled, he asked, "What's wrong with you?"

Those words caught my attention, and I realized I was the one with a problem. Jason was the victim of my misdirected frustration.

Sound familiar? Does to me.

ᴥ Reflections

PATSY'S GRAPHIC EXAMPLE of a jumbled mass of rubber bands of emotions fits many of us at times. When we're in that state, we can't find any blessings mixed in with those red, blue, green, and yellow rubber bands. We can't even figure out why we're angry and confused, much less see good woven throughout it.

Patsy gives us the encouragement we need that we can sort through those jumbled emotions with God's help. It may happen through the unexpected comment of a loved one—even though it bothers us they're so smart. God may minister to us through therapy, the pastor's sermon, exercise, or journaling. Whatever it takes, we need to look for the underlying causes and then pay attention to how God unravels those rubber bands.

How big is your rubber band mass of emotions? Does God want you to do something about unwinding them? You'll find unexpected blessings if you do.

❦ Journal

✒ Journal

. . . *there is a friend who sticks closer than a brother.*

PROVERBS 18:24

A Faithful Friend

Joan Clayton

"I'VE COME TO CHECK MARY OUT," my student's dad replied. "She's going to live with her real mother on the west coast," he added.

"No! No! No!" Everything within me wanted to scream. "You can't let Mary go. She is just now beginning to excel and adjust to school in every way." If only people could see into little children's hearts.

My heart ached. Mary's beautiful big brown eyes looked into mine with such pain. Tears rolled down her little chubby cheeks as she hugged me as far as she could reach.

I asked Mary's dad if I might have a few minutes to say good-bye. I took Mary into my arms and held her close. Her tiny frame heaved sobs of sorrow and I prayed for words to soothe and comfort her.

"Remember when we had a new student come to our classroom and I assigned you to be a special friend?" Mary nodded.

"Well, there will be a special friend in your new classroom. He will be with you always. You will never be alone," I explained.

Mary questioned hopefully, "Is that for real, Teacher?"

"Yes, Mary," I replied. "You can bet your life on it, because I will never stop praying for you. I pray that this special friend will keep His angels watching over you all of your days."

Mary stopped crying. "Teacher, I love you," she said as she brushed away her tears.

"I love you, too," my voice quivered as I held and hugged her one last time.

Mary took her daddy's hand and walked out of my life that balmy spring day in April, 1981.

Ten years later, in May of 1991, an unexpected blessing gently knocked on my classroom door. My class had just returned from noon recess and were all settled around me for story time. One of the children ran to answer the door. A beautiful young lady entered the room, smiling at me.

I smiled back and said, "Please have a seat and I will be with you in a moment." I finished my story and assigned the next task to the children.

As I approached the young lady, she smiled again and said: "Do you remember me, Mrs. Clayton? I'm Mary."

It was then that I recognized those big, beautiful, brown eyes that were now gazing into mine with such love and admiration.

"Mary! It's you!" I exclaimed, only this time I was crying. "What a thrill and a blessing to see you. You are all grown up."

Mary began to speak with great excitement. "Do you remember holding me close that day I left your classroom? You told me that I would have a special friend who would never leave me. And guess what Mrs. Clayton? I did! This faithful friend guided me all through school. He has made a way for me to go to college on a scholarship and become a teacher like you. Jesus answered your prayers for me."

What an unexpected blessing came to me that day. Thirty one years of teaching brought me many blessings indeed, and those children could never escape my love or my prayers. I may not always see the results of my prayers as dramatic as my prayers for Mary, but I know they are answered just the same.

Just a few simple words made such a blessed difference.

❧ Reflections

WE MAY NEVER KNOW the impact our words have upon others. Joan was fortunate to have the unexpected blessing of seeing the results of her words and prayers. Mary took the time and effort to share how Joan's love had affected her. Both were blessed. You and I can be blessed by faith as we know God uses our words and prayers to make a difference in others' lives. And we can take the time to communicate our gratitude to those who have brought joy, comfort, encouragement, or peace into our lives because of their words or actions.

Is there someone who has made a difference in your life and you haven't yet thanked them or acknowledged their impact? Write or call them today. Are they "on-line?" A quick E-mail message may not be formal, but they'll still receive an unexpected blessing from your words.

Journal

Journal

Then you will know the truth, and the truth will set you free.

JOHN 8:32

The Blessings Of Truth

Bill Hybels

In THE EARLY YEARS OF OUR MARRIAGE, both Lynne and I chose peacekeeping over truth telling. I was starting up a church and I had a lot of upheaval at work—no money, no people, no buildings, and plenty of disagreement among those who were involved with the project. Lynne had troubles of her own at home. She was pregnant; we had two boarders living with us who took a great deal of her time; and she was teaching flute lessons to help make ends meet. So with upheaval at home and upheaval at work, we had a common understanding whenever we got together—"Don't make any more waves." Nevertheless, inside us the frustrations were building up.

God began to work on Lynne's heart. Before long, my tender-hearted wife started meeting me at the door saying, "Sit down, I have to tell you something. I haven't been truthful with you. I am sick and tired of being tenth on your priority list. You don't show me much affection. I don't like the way this marriage is heading, and I'm not going to stand for it."

I did not respond very well. I did not say, "I'm glad to hear what's on your heart. I'll change my schedule and start thinking about your needs as well as my own." Instead I yelled, "With all the problems I have trying to start this church—and you lay this trip on me! What do you want, anyway? Here, take some blood."

In spite of my reaction, Lynne stuck to her guns. She knew our marriage needed work and she decided to fight until I saw the light. Over the years God used Lynne's tough love until I faced the truth about myself and allowed him to do a lot of surgery on me.

But then, once I started listening to Lynne and working on my problems, I began seeing some things in her I did not want to live with anymore. Having learned the value of truth telling, I decided to open up. "Sweetheart," I said, "I see a streak of self-centeredness in your life that bothers me."

Sweet, softhearted Lynne did not say, "Thank you for sharing your feelings." Instead she ran away sobbing, "I can't believe you'd say that!" and slammed the bedroom door. But I stuck to my guns, and we had several more rough months. Eventually she made some changes, just as I had had to do, and our marriage became peaceful once again. But this time there was a difference. This was not a counterfeit peace based on avoiding the real issues. This was the peace of the Lord—based on truth, real and lasting.

Reflections

TRUTH HURTS SOME TIMES. We don't like to hear it! We run from it! But Lynne and Bill have given us a powerful example that if we'll work through the pain, we can discover greater peace. It will become a source of great blessings because the dross of our lives will be refined. We'll become more like Jesus and what greater, unexpected blessing can there be than that? It'll be worth it, if we'll just give up, give in, and give out. We need to give up our wrong ideas that we assume are "truth." We must give in to God's definition of truth. And we can give out truth in gentle, small portions. We won't be sorry we did. Just ask Bill and Lynne.

In what way can you "give up, give in, and give out" truth to bring greater blessings in your life and relationships today?

Journal

Journal

Do you have eyes but fail to see, and ears but fail to hear?

MARK 8:18a

Nearsighted "Krischans"

Tina Krause

THE LETTER FROM MY NEW FRIEND READ: "I am surely happy that we have tourists like you two visiting our shores. Some tourists come here only to have fun and to block their minds from the other aspects of Jamaican life . . ."

If she only knew.

The travel brochures boasted tropical beaches and dining in the moonlight to the rhythm of a calypso band. But sightseeing included more unexpected views than we had anticipated or desired to see.

Our first glimpse occurred on the drive to the hotel as the bus snaked through the coastal villages en route to Ocho Rios. Cardboard shacks with tin roofs dotted the landscape; children played in rudimental, germ-infested surroundings; and mothers bathed their babies in makeshift tubs, perched atop crates in dirt backyards.

The "four-star" hotel accommodations were below average by U.S. standards and we strained to walk through town without the locals harassing us for business. A ten-year-old boy solicited buyers for his handmade yo-yos. On the same street corner a drug dealer openly pushed narcotics repeating, "Hey M'on, I've got good stuff," as we passed by. Meanwhile, a self-ascribed hairdresser trailed us, begging for business. "Hey lady, I braid your hair, I braid your hair . . ."

Unaccustomed to their aggressiveness, I was both startled and annoyed. Raised in an all white Midwestern town, I had few encounters with the "less fortunate." Yet I never considered myself guilty of prejudice or discrimination. A culture steeped in poverty proved me wrong.

On the first night of our Jamaican vacation, more than feelings of human benevolence prompted me to pray. It was a plea of survival.

"Get me out of this God-forsaken country, Lord," I lamented inside my hotel room. Yet by my prayer's end, I acquiesced to my surroundings saying, "Lord, these people are difficult to take, but while I'm here, help me to see them through your eyes."

Afterward, I forgot my prayer. God remembered.

Several days passed and we again strolled the cluttered streets of Ocho Rios on our way to the marketplace. Nothing had changed, except this time my heart lightened as an indelible smile covered my face, though I couldn't explain why.

Again, the drug pusher approached us but this time, without intimidation, we did the talking. "No, thanks," I said, "We don't need drugs, we get high on Jesus." The tall black man with stooped shoulders raised his hand and shook his head as he walked away to rejoin his friends. "Ah, you Krischans," he replied with his Jamaican accent, indicating he had met our kind before.

As we approached the boy merchant, we stopped to purchase several yo-yos and chat awhile. I searched my purse for a children's Bible tract as we asked him about his schooling, his home life and if he knew who Jesus was. Suddenly, a crowd of Jamaicans surrounded us to listen as we shared the love of God.

Throughout the afternoon, the people I shunned a few days before, became our biggest blessing as we spoke with vendors, taxi drivers, and whomever crossed our path. On the street we met a Jamaican woman named Bev, a single mom who worked for the Jamaican government.

After we conversed for some time, we agreed to write to one another and I assured her I'd send packages from home filled with items she and her son, Jaime, couldn't obtain in the West Indies.

As we made our way back to the hotel we encountered the drug pusher again. This time—though surrounded by his friends—he yelled to us from an abandoned building, his voice echoing through the streets.

"Hey Krischans! Krischans!" As we turned toward him, his voice softened. "Please . . . pray for me."

Jesus said, *Your eyes are to see with—why don't you look? Why don't you open your ears and listen?* . . . Mark 8:18 (TLB). Prior to that day I was blind. I chose to deny the unmistakable truth—that lower classes of people and unfamiliar cultures frightened and, in some instances, repelled me. As a result, like so many Americans who have been sheltered from races and cultures apart from their own, I suffered from spiritual nearsightedness.

Yet by the time I left Jamaica, my fondness for its people intensified. God performed corrective eye surgery on me and I knew the people of Ocho Rios viewed me differently too. Bev's letter confirmed that.

For somewhere between a prayer and an encounter, I was unexpectedly transformed into more than just another insensitive American tourist.

I was a "Krischan" who had her Father's eyes.

❧ Reflections

JUST LIKE TINA, it's easy for us to have blinded eyes to the needs of others. We easily see things from our own perspective and forget that God has a more complete one. He loves all the people of the world, though we may feel uncomfortable in another culture. Tina had the unexpected blessing of having her eyes opened to the international God of the universe and His great love for every single human on the face of the earth. "Go into all the world," we're commanded, not just the ones that feel comfortable. If we do, we'll also, like Tina, see God's unexpected blessings.

How do other cultures make you uncomfortable? Pray for a foreign country and have your eyes opened to the unexpected blessing of an expanded love for the world.

Journal

Journal

Journal

No discipline seems pleasant at the time, but painful. Later on, however, it produces a harvest of righteousness and peace for those who have been trained by it.

HEBREWS 12:11

Unexpected
Self Worth

Gary Smalley

SEVENTEEN-YEAR-OLD DENISE challenged me after a seminar, stating that she knew there were no benefits in the things she'd endured. "I'm always looking for the first exception," I said to her. "Why don't we sit down and you tell me your problems."

I quickly learned from Denise that she hated four things about her life: she believed she was ugly, stupid, and overweight, and she was convinced her parents were unfair.

"Do you want God's best in your life?" I asked her.

"Yes," she answered.

"What do you think God's best is?"

"I really don't know."

"God's best and highest will is for us to love (value) Him with all our hearts, and to love (value) others as ourselves. Do you realize that you have everything you need to fulfill God's will and experience His best in your life?"

"And just how can I find it?" she inquired.

We started with her problems concerning her physical appearance. I asked her if she wanted to be beautiful.

"Of course!" she snapped.

I explained that a humble attitude was the key to physical beauty because God gives His grace to the humble. I suggested that she pray a prayer like this: "Lord, thank You that through love You can give me spiritual beauty that will reflect on my physical appearance. I thank You that as You teach me how to love You and others, people will begin to see Your beauty in me."

Then I suggested that perhaps God was using her appearance to protect her. Because of her appearance, men would not be attracted to her for purely physical reasons, and she would not be tempted to use her appearance to manipulate people. So in any relationship, whether friendship or romance, she would know the person was attracted to her because of her inner, lasting qualities that only God could develop within her.

She smiled for the first time, and her smile revealed a pretty face. Simply relaxing her facial muscles immediately made her more attractive. When a person can thank God for the good they know is there but cannot yet see, facial expressions often change and others can see a new beauty and calm.

I went on to explain that self-hatred might be the cause of her overeating. If she started to relax and began to like herself, the compulsion to overeat might subside. But even if she could not lose weight, she could still find her fulfillment in God.

Denise's below-average intelligence also held a disguised benefit. Denise had never battled with God over theological issues. For her, a childlike faith was more natural. Although asking God difficult questions about our faith is not wrong, there is value in simple faith, as Jesus showed when He used a child as an example.

As we talked, Denise realized this was true. She told me of a number of times when students at her high school had sought her counsel because she was known for being trusting and for having above-average common sense.

We then considered Denise's relationship with her parents. Any support she received from them was based solely on her achievements, which were few. Denise believed they preferred her brother because he excelled in athletics and earned good grades in school. The concept of unconditional love and affection was foreign to the family. Her father traveled extensively, which Denise resented, and her mother complained about having to raise the kids without his help.

Each of these trials had its benefits. Because Denise felt unloved, her sensitivity to others from similar homes was unusually strong. I explained how that sensitivity could, if she would let it, enable her to reach out to others, to accept them as they are, and to understand their needs. Her parents' favoritism revealed the futility and frustration of expecting people to make her happy. Learning this could lead her into a closer relationship with Christ, who would never leave her or forsake her. And her father's frequent absences turned out to be the greatest benefit of all. Her need for a father was the major factor that brought her to faith in Christ. And finally, her poor relationship with her parents could make her more sensitive to her own children when she married.

Denise skipped away from our meeting with a smile on her face. Several years after our meeting she sent me a letter telling me what good things God was continuing to do in her life. She had gone on to college, majored in sociology, and become a social worker helping the handicapped. Her trials, she said, produced the patience she needed for this kind of work, so now she too helps people discover treasure in their trials. The more love she gives, the more her self-worth soars.

Reflections

GARY WISELY HELPED DENISE recognize the unexpected blessings in the very things that she thought were her greatest liabilities. Her eyes had been closed to the loving motives behind God's plan for her. Our eyes can easily be blinded to the same thing when we only focus on the disadvantages of our physical, emotional, or spiritual condition. If our vision only focuses on the negative, the positive will be cloudy.

It may seem like a cross too heavy to bear, but God will reveal a beautiful purpose that far outweighs the burden. Like Denise, we can concentrate on the assets behind every seeming hindrance. It's all a matter of perspective. God's blessings are just waiting to be recognized.

What liability or disadvantage have you been concentrating on? What blessings will you acknowledge instead? Let yourself be surprised with God's unexpected blessings.

Journal

Journal

Journal

Let us not become weary in doing good, for at the proper time we will reap a harvest if we do not give up.

GALATIANS 6:9

Join The Club

Georgia Curtis Ling

IT FINALLY HAPPENED. The Mommy honeymoon was over. And it was so close to Mother's Day. Our son declared us, "The Meanest Parents In The World."

Yes. We have now joined the ranks of the battle-scared Meanest Parents In The World Club. For short, let's call it the MPW Club.

With bent eyebrows, folded arms and stomping feet, our five-year-old awarded us this recognition when we wouldn't allow him to watch a particular cartoon. (I might add, that it is not fit for children, adults, or monkeys to watch.) He also added that other parents let their kids watch it.

I almost swallowed my tongue as I tried to contain my laughter. His normal sparkling eyes only contained sparks of frustration and anger as he asked, "How can you be such mean parents?" Instantaneously, I flashed back to my younger days when I blurted out those same words to my parents. So, of course, the first thing that came out of my mouth was, "It runs in the family. When I was a kid, I had the meanest parents in the world, too. But don't worry, we'll grow out of it."

I think my parents were the founding members of the MPW Club.

We weren't allowed to wear make-up or date until we were sixteen. Our curfew was 9:30 p.m.—until my sister and her boyfriend broke it and then they moved it to 9 p.m. (Why go out if you had to be in before dark?)

They wouldn't let us watch the popular show "Laugh In" or anything with GoGo Dancing. They were afraid of the negative influence it might have.

If sports or other extra curricular activities conflicted with

Youth Group or church, guess which one came first? You guessed it: church.

I just know I was cursed with the meanest parents in the world. Mom and Dad must have renewed and paid their membership dues every year because they never changed. But thank goodness, I grew out of that mind-set and finally realized the curse was actually a blessing in disguise. I found out for myself that when kids call it mean—God calls it love and protection. When other parents call it overprotection—God commands parents to instruct their children in His ways, not the ways of the world. When teens want to do their own thing—the Scripture lays out moral absolutes that parents are instructed to teach.

At the time, I wasn't real enthused with my parents, but now I thank God I was blessed with the meanest parents in the world. I wear my new title with pride. I promise to pay my dues and renew my membership every year to the Meanest Parents In The World Club.

Join the club. Some day your children will recognize it's an unexpected blessing.

ᯤ Reflections

AH, PARENTING. One of the most difficult, yet blessed, roles in the world. Like Georgia discovered, parents are appreciated when they do what their child wants, and are rewarded with temper tantrums when they don't. A child has no comprehension of the intense love we have for them, and so many of us are co-members with Georgia (and her parents) of the MPW Club. Someday, though, we will receive the unexpected blessing of a child who *rises up and calls her blessed* (Proverbs 31:28). Georgia did, I did, and we can trust God that our children will. Later, they will think we resigned from the Club, when actually, they have just given up their own membership in the "Immature Children of the World Club." Until then, we can continue to be those mean parents because of our great love for them.

ᯤ

Are you discouraged today because your children don't appreciate or approve your parenting methods? Join the MPW Club. Someday your membership will bring great benefits.

Journal

✑ Journal

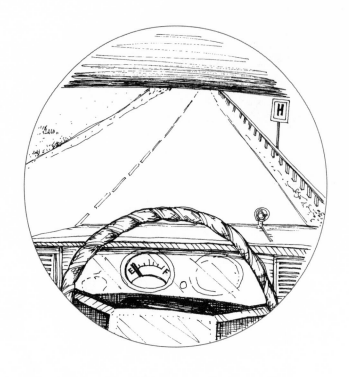

. . . I was a stranger and you let me in.

MATTHEW 25:35c

A Double Blessing

Gail Gaymer Martin

A COUPLE OF SUMMERS AGO, my husband and I made a trip out West, stopping in Salt Lake City to visit Temple Square. We reminded ourselves as we parked our car that we needed to fill the gas tank before we left the city. But with the strains of the wonderful organ concert ringing in our ears, we searched for the freeway entrance and headed toward California—and the Great Salt Flats.

Then the empty light glowed from the dashboard and we looked at each other in panic. We were too far from Salt Lake City to turn back and before us lay the desolate stretch of highway. "No Service" signs marked every exit and as we approached our last hope, we took the off-ramp with panic.

But our worst fear was realized: a "No Service" sign stood at the top. We faced fifty miles of nothing and a near empty gas tank. Strangely enough, another car sat at the top of the ramp and upon investigation, the driver was a young man who said he was resting. "Resting," we said. "What a strange place to rest." The heat of the desert shimmered on the pure white salt fields below us.

The stranger offered gas from his tank, but we had no siphon. Then he said, "I'll be happy to follow you. If you run out of gas, I'll take you to a station and bring you back."

We looked at each other in panic. Was this some roadside scam? Could we be mugged or worse—killed? Dear Lord, please keep us safe. We had no choice but to accept the stranger's offer. We pulled away with him following close behind. Our "empty" light glowed, as we flew along the highway.

As if God had given us a heavenly supply of gasoline, we saw the Bonneville Speedway like a speck in the distance. The AAA map showed a gas station there. The stranger followed behind. The further we drove, the more we felt ashamed for our untrusting thoughts about him, but his presence gave us a sense of security.

On gasoline fumes, we pulled into the station with prayers of thanksgiving soaring to heaven. The stranger waved as if to leave, but we called him back.

"Here is some money as a token of our appreciation. We felt so good having you there."

"No, no," he said, shaking his head.

I approached him, my eyes pleading. "Please take the money. Your presence behind us was a blessing. I must admit, I have never prayed so much in my life."

"Let me tell you a funny story," he said. "When your husband approached my car, I was resting, but praying too. My sister is ill, and I am driving to see her empty-handed. I put every penny I had into the gas tank. You've answered my prayer."

As he took our offer, we realized God had unexpectedly blessed us all.

❧ Reflections

WE NEVER KNOW HOW GOD is going to answer our prayers. In His creative sovereignty, He can intertwine the lives of many. Sometimes, we must get to the very bottom of the tank before we seek the Lord and depend upon Him. Then, as Gail discovered in the midst of a crisis, He comes through—in a totally unexpected way. And He won't just bless us, He'll bless many . . . because of our great God's knowledge of everyone's needs. As He's blessing you, look around. You may see that others are being blessed simultaneously. He's good at that.

❧

How has God unexpectedly blessed you while also blessing others? He may have done it more than you've noticed or others have said. Look for it the next time you're given a blessing.

Journal

Journal

*Delight yourself in the LORD and he will
give you the desires of your heart.*

PSALM 37:4

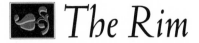 # The Rim

Patricia Mora

I HAD BEEN CRYING for days. Nothing made sense. We had obeyed God's commands. I had quit my job and stayed home—through financial trials and frustration. After nearly five years of difficulties, my husband had a decent job. We could finally afford to buy this little house we had been renting—but the owner had just sold it out from under us. "Why, Lord?"

It wasn't perfect. It was tiny, with a barely decent sized "master" bedroom and two other bedrooms best described as miniature. If I could have my "druthers"—which I knew I could not—I would buy a bigger house, adding a two car garage, a pantry in the kitchen and one more room for our small business.

Why another trial? What have we done? Is there some sin in our lives? We could think of none.

The owner of this tiny house had promised to wait for the paperwork to go through. We knew low income government programs took an inordinate amount of time, but this one had dragged on and on. As the months passed, I had updated the information we were receiving from the agency to reassure the owner that buying this house was just a few more weeks away. He had never indicated he was growing tired of waiting. The phone call had come out of nowhere, knocking the breath right out of me.

Even though this little house was far less than we needed, I really loved it. I liked the floor plan and the large closets. I loved the "big" kitchen—the only normal-sized room in the house. Most of all, I loved the neighborhood. It was surrounded by tall pines and Oregon grape undergrowth. Huge ferns grew wild and blooming rhododendrons blazed scarlet, purple, and white.

Here the silence and majesty of God's creation brought peace in the midst of distress.

Our little rental was hidden, tucked away in the forest, in a tract of homes aptly named "Wilderness Rim," some 1200 feet above sea level. From my windows, I watched birds and butterflies play in the sun. Dusk and dawn brought deer to the edge of the cul-de-sac, as chipmunks chirped their high-pitched cries.

How can I leave this neighborhood where God has given us such peace? Oh, why, Lord? Why did you let this tiny haven be sold out from under us?

We had to find a new place to live. The government program was useless now. We would simply have to rent—again. Brokenhearted, confused with God's unfathomable plan, we drove down the mountain to seek a new rental house. Hoping to stay in the "Rim," we entered the only real estate office in town.

Disappointed, we learned there were few rentals in the "Rim" at any time. None, now. There was, however, a single house for sale, just listed that morning. The out-of-town owner would sell VA. To our surprise, my veteran husband could qualify for this house, using a "no down/no closing" loan—if we were interested in buying. Did we want to see the house?

We did. Driving back up to the Rim, we pulled into the familiar subdivision to view the only house for sale. With pleasure, we discovered this house had exactly the same floor plan as our rental—with a few exceptions: it had a pantry in the kitchen, a two-car garage, and a bonus room large enough for our business. Everything I'd wanted added to our rental. Best of all, this house had nearly the same view as the little one I loved. That's because it was right next door.

God was not angry with us. He only wanted to bless us with something better—an unexpected blessing.

✑ *Reflections*

WHEN THE DARK SEEMS DARKEST, God may only be bringing an early morning dawn. When hope seems distant, God may only be preparing a way for an improved road to blessings. Patricia couldn't understand why God wouldn't meet their needs. We've all felt that way. We easily conclude that God doesn't care or maybe He doesn't have the required power. Then suddenly He bursts forth with a plan that blesses us far more than we could ever anticipate. He does care! He does love! His arm is not too short! Even when He doesn't answer our cries exactly the way we desire, He still knows the better plan. Watch for the dawn and the road signs. He's planning blessings all along the way.

Is there a need in your life that hasn't been fulfilled? Does it seem too dark to continue praying? Don't give up. God's unexpected blessing may be just around the corner.

Journal

Journal

For in the day of trouble he will keep me safe in his dwelling; he will hide me in the shelter of his tabernacle and set me high upon a rock.

PSALM 27:5, 6

Through The Flood

Sharyn McDonald

After months of fund raisers, garage sales, prayer and anticipation, the day had finally arrived in the summer of 1997. All across the nation, parents, just like us, were watching their teens leave home for IYC (International Youth Conference) in Fort Collins, Colorado. Our 22-year-old daughter and 18-year-old son were among the thousands of junior high through college aged students who converged on Colorado State University to attend the conference. It was an exciting time and the week was filled with great speakers, worship and praise, classes, concerts, and activities. God moved mightily in the hearts of many of those attending. Although, to California kids, it seemed to rain a great deal of the time, nothing as insignificant as a little rain could dampen their enthusiasm. Little did any of us know that what began as a gentle rain would soon become a raging torrent of destruction.

Each night, after the meeting, the kids enjoyed a special concert. On one particular night, rather than dismiss the meeting, the leaders sensed the Holy Spirit telling them to wait. Everyone was told to remain in the building and to give the Lord time to minister to their hearts. Concerned about the concert, the kids were told that it would start a little later and asked for just a few more minutes of their time.

Ten minutes later a wall of destruction crashed through the campus laying waste to all in its path and destroying the hall where the kids would have been if they had been dismissed on time. If the leaders had not been receptive and obedient to the voice of the Holy Spirit, if the youth had not been obedient to their exhortation to wait upon the Lord, hundreds of kids would have been trapped within the flooded basement of the concert venue, or swept away in the raging torrent. Countless lives would have been lost and families devastated by the loss of their children.

The flood cut a path of destruction through the town. All across the nation, the news media carried stories of loss and devastation. Lives were lost, homes and property were destroyed, hundreds were left homeless. Yet in the midst of the massive destruction, not one of the kids at IYC died or was seriously injured. While the flood waters raged, they huddled together for warmth and encouraged each other with prayer and songs of praise. They endured through the night and twelve hours later emerged into the morning light, to a scene of devastation and a city that had suffered tremendously. God had covered them with His love and sheltered them with His protection.

Although they were exhausted, hundreds of the teens and their youth leaders volunteered to help the community with rescue and clean up, working side by side with the flood victims. Before they left Fort Collins, IYC took a special offering for the flood victims and thousands of dollars were presented to the city as a gift from the youth.

We all welcomed our children home with hearts filled with thanksgiving and praise for the unexpected blessings of God's love and protection. He truly set their feet on dry ground and their hearts on His unfailing love. He continues to bless me as both my children have grown stronger in the Lord since the flood.

ᴥ Reflections

GOD IS AWESOME. He works far above our human minds can fathom. His love is immeasurable and He only wants to bless. Sharyn never could have anticipated how His unfailing nature would be manifested as she said good-bye to her two children. If she had known the possible danger, she might have blocked God's work. Trusting our great God to do what He wants brings deeper blessings: lives changed, hearts bonded, generosity demonstrated. Only He knows the results He desires, we just need to trust Him.

ᴥ

Are you hesitating taking a risk because God's plan isn't completely evident and you haven't approved it yet? If He gives you instructions, follow them. Only He knows the deeper, unexpected blessings He has in mind.

Journal

Journal

Can a mother forget the baby at her breast and have no compassion on the child she has borne? Though she may forget, I will never forget you! See, I have engraved you on the palms of my hands; your walls are ever before me.

ISAIAH 49:15, 16

Expressing Needed Love

Josh McDowell

I SPOKE TO A LARGE NUMBER of teenagers at Fishnet, a large outdoor music festival and teaching conference held on a farm in Virginia. One morning while speaking about the importance and value of saving sex for marriage, I told the young people in the crowd of about twelve thousand that they were special, and to never forget that they had immeasurable worth, and that someone who truly loved them would recognize that worth and honor it by waiting for marriage to have sex.

Later that morning I noticed a young blonde girl, about twelve years old, following me. I stopped and asked, "Did you want to see me?"

She replied rather shyly, "Do you really think I'm special?"

"Yes!" I answered vehemently. "God made you special and don't you ever forget it." I cautiously put my arms around her shoulders and gave her a tender fatherly hug. She suddenly burst into tears.

"You don't know how long I've waited for that," she said. "My mom and dad divorced five years ago, and my dad has never hugged me or told me I'm special."

Five days later as I left for the airport, a note was slipped to me by a security man who said a little girl wanted me to have it. The tightly folded note had just six words written in red:

Thank you for loving me . . . Koreen.

That young woman was crying out for love and acceptance, the kind that only a father could give, the kind she had never received.

❧ Reflections

NOT ALL PARENTS give their children the love and acceptance they need. Josh was able to give a momentary burst of hope and love to Koreen, but only the Lord will be able to fill her to overflowing. God designed parents to be a blessing to their children, but in their own neediness, they focus on themselves rather on the needs of their children.

Yet we can know our Heavenly Father's love. He sent His most valuable Son, Jesus, to die on a Cross for each one of us. That unselfish act demonstrated God's love as no other act can.

God loves you! He'll never stop loving you! You are unconditionally accepted! Be blessed by those truths. He wants you to experience His love, even when others fail you.

Do you know God's unconditional love for you? If so, enjoy. If not, ask Him to come into your heart and life right now and know that because of His love for you, He has indeed become your Lord and Savior.

Journal

✑ Journal

_____

_____

_____

_____

_____

_____

_____

_____

_____

_____

_____

_____

_____

_____

_____

_____

_____

_____

_____

_____

Journal

Finally, brothers, whatever is true, whatever is noble, whatever is right, whatever is pure, whatever is lovely, whatever is admirable—if anything is excellent or praiseworthy— think about such things.

PHILLIPIANS 4:8

Discovering Gold In The Golden Years

Mary Beth Nelson

As I ENTER A NEW PERIOD of life when it's time to get the cholesterol down and the thyroid up, when arthritic threats become dominant with stiffer joints, I find myself wondering, "Where is the gold in the golden years?" After a rather sleepless night, I pondered this "golden" question while pouring a second cup of coffee.

I realize everything in this life is not perfect, nor should perfection be expected. The bones will eventually become brittle, and the muscles may not work as well as they once did. But are those the things on which God really wants me to concentrate? When I complain, am I asking for my will to be done instead of His?

I know everything good that happens to me comes from the Lord. It is more difficult to appreciate negative occurrences until I remind myself that the negative can produce blessings. Ross W. Marrs once said, "Take away my capacity for pain, and you rob me of the possibility for joy."

While indulging in a third cup of coffee, images of energetic grandsons and beautiful granddaughters suddenly popped into my mind. The sight of our lovely granddaughter in her bridal gown a few weeks earlier sparked a reality of fleeting years. At the same time, her radiant happiness brought new warmth to my heart, not to mention her request that I play her Wedding

March. Could that possibly be a fraction of the gold I'm looking for?

Another granddaughter expressed a desire for her first little girl to bear my name. Even though this idea is susceptible to change, her thought made the "gold" a little shinier.

When I actually consider the blessings God provides to ease my aching body, the list becomes endless. Enjoying more time with nature's elements through a flower's budding, a bird's melody, falling snowflakes, and smell of refreshing rain; unexpectedly hearing from cherished friends with whom younger years were shared; expressions of love and appreciation from daughters even as they tend to their own family matters; treasured memories of a son whose earthly life ended during his younger years; the eyes of a great-grandchild asking nothing but a smile and a little love; and best of all, a faithful, loving, caring husband who still enjoys a picnic for two by the windmill as well as occasional candlelight suppers in the dining room.

Unexpected gold in the golden years? It is there if I will only take time to recognize it. God has promised its possibility. The blessed probability is up to me.

❧ Reflections

NONE OF US CHERISH the idea of growing old. We fear the aches and pains. We wonder what ailments will diminish our creativity and productivity. Mary Beth has comforted us with the assurance that though some of the difficulties may try to steal our joy, we can concentrate on God's blessings. We'll never be able to prepare for those years, other than developing now our ability to focus on those things which are true, noble, right, pure, lovely, and admirable. Maturing that habit now will strengthen our attitude muscles to keep focused on God later. As a result, our vision will appreciate the unexpected blessings that only come with advancing age.

What do you fear about growing older? What blessings can only result from being in that time of life? Though there may be difficulties during that age, trust that God has blessings you cannot fathom right now.

Journal

Journal

In his heart a man plans his course, but the LORD determines his steps.

PROVERBS 16:9

Appointment In Honduras

Susan Kimmel Wright

THE TELEPHONE'S CLAMOR shattered my morning fog. We'd been in the mountainous Honduran capital, Tegucigalpa, for the past three weeks, adopting baby Francisca. Between her and our toddler Tony, who we'd adopted there two years before, it had been one in a series of sleepless nights.

I fumbled the receiver to my ear.

Our attorney's voice greeted me, "Good morning. Now is probably not a good time to ask you, but would you be interested in another baby?"

I was still in my pajamas. Francisca, in my arms, had finished her morning bottle and wet her diaper. Tony sat at the breakfast table, making a mess of his cornflakes.

"Who is it?" My husband Dave uneasily considered my stunned expression.

I held him off as I listened to the lawyer. "Tony's birthmother delivered a baby girl this past week. She needs to place the baby for adoption. I thought immediately of you. That way they can grow up together," he concluded, his voice bright. Obviously, he had had a good night's rest.

I explained to Dave. Despite—and maybe because of—this sense of something huge and overwhelming washing over us, we scarcely hesitated.

"When can we pick her up? Tomorrow?"

"Oh no, you come get her this afternoon."

Everything was happening so fast. Two years ago we'd been

childless. As of 8:30 this morning, we were parents of three. Our new little car, back in the States, was suddenly one seatbelt short.

We weren't entirely sure how we'd survive three children under age three. But this was clearly a divinely arranged appointment. Here we were in Honduras, thousands of miles from home, just in time for this baby's arrival. And later that day, when we met tiny Daisy, we learned she'd made her appearance a month early, seemingly just so she wouldn't miss us.

If Daisy had arrived just a little earlier, we'd have missed her altogether, or perhaps we'd have received her instead of Francisca. But God had wanted us to have them both.

The next two years passed in a blur of exhaustion, diapers, and bottles. But it also passed quickly—a time of toothless smiles, first words, and wobbly steps. Our arms were full at last—full of threefold blessings, one unexpectedly.

❧ Reflections

YOU JUST NEVER KNOW what God has on the drawing board! We make our plans, seeking the Lord, but He may surprise us with an added bonus, an unexpected blessing. Susan and her husband unhesitantly obeyed God's call and their family was complete. They had no idea God had a slightly different plan than they'd originally anticipated. Yet, now with a threefold blessing, they can't imagine it any other way.

Yes, we do need to plan. We do need to seek God. But He isn't obligated to reveal the complete blueprint from the beginning. He opens the doors and we walk through. But there just may be an added bonus we didn't expect. Don't worry, it'll only be a blessing.

Have you sometimes concluded you must not have obeyed God because the plan changed later? It may not be that you were disobedient, just that God had an unexpected addition to the blueprint. Trust Him.

Journal

Journal

*For the eyes of the LORD range throughout
the earth to strengthen those whose hearts are
fully committed to him.*

II Chronicles 16:9

When Jesus Came Home For Christmas

Jeanne Zornes

THIS IS A STORY from the *St. Louis Post-Dispatch* about a little weather-beaten plastic "Jesus" figure, which was kidnapped from an outdoor nativity scene in Missouri.

It happened some time during the night of the 1993 Christmas season as little plastic Jesus lay in a crib under the unseeing eye of the equally battered "Mary," her head bashed from some accident in the storage shed.

When its owner, Ted, noticed the baby missing, he found a note. Jesus was taking a vacation, it said, and would be back on Christmas Eve in 1994.

Nobody knew who did the joke abduction. But Ted had lots of friends who knew his love of celebrating Christmas. Sometimes he'd even play Christmas songs on family trips—in the summer. And for fifteen years, he'd set up the same outdoor nativity scene.

That year, Ted started getting post cards and letters signed "Jesus" from Colorado, Arizona, California, Texas, and Montana. The messages had different handwriting and styles. Some letters had photos, like the ones from South Padre, Texas, showing Jesus sitting on a surf board and claiming he'd taken windsurfing lessons.

Finally came a letter from Juneau, saying "Jesus" would be visiting friends at the North Pole before coming home for Christmas.

The continuing prank entertained Ted enormously. He could hardly wait for Christmas.

Then, that fall, Ted got sick. Real sick. Within weeks, he died.

The post cards from "Jesus" stopped for a while. Then a note came to Ted's widow, Liz. "Took some time off from my vacation to make sure Ted got settled in," the note read. "He's just fine. See you soon. Love, Jesus."

Christmas Eve came. Liz cleaned her house as expectation ran high. Neighbors and friends went on alert. One family stayed home from a party, another kept looking out the window.

About 6 p.m. a baffled driver knocked on Liz's door. In his back seat, wrapped in a white hooded baby towel, lay the plastic Jesus he'd just picked up at the airport. Next to it, a tiny pink suitcase decorated with teddy bears.

Liz excitedly returned the figurine to the crib. The suitcase was opened. In it were souvenirs from all the places the figurine had traveled like Mickey Mouse sunglasses, a University of Wisconsin tee-shirt, and a package of salt from Salt Lake City. A card inside read: "Please accept these symbols of love and share them with those who need to keep the spirit of Christmas."

"Who would have known that a friendly prank could become an unexpected Christmas Eve blessing to a widow in Missouri."

ஜ Reflections

THE LORD GOD ALMIGHTY is aware of all of our needs, even before we have them. The first Christmas after a loved one dies can be a tough one. But Jesus knows the pain of loss—and He offers the grieving one the best gift possible: Himself. Jeanne writes of a widow whose heart was comforted through a prank that God intended for an even greater purpose than the prankster could ever imagine. As this surprising story shows us, He may offer Himself in a most unusual way. And it will bring unexpected blessings to many. We can praise God for His creativity.

Are you experiencing some loss? Jesus knows and cares. He will reveal more about Himself through your grief. Look for His blessings in an unexpected way.

Journal

Journal

. . . and a little child will lead them.

ISAIAH 11:6b

God's Little Messenger

Maria Faulconer

"**Y**OU'RE NOTHING BUT A FAILURE!" The words rumbled around in my head as I struggled to put words on paper. I was seated in an alcove at a fast food restaurant fretting over an article I was writing. For the past two years, I'd been snatching precious moments to write between teaching and raising two teenagers, and nothing was working. My words had no passion, no spark. Why was I even bothering?

As I swished the dregs of my lukewarm coffee in a halfhearted motion, a tiny figure in pink plopped herself down on the seat across from me. She couldn't have been more than two years old, but her presence filled the room. She smiled, a joyful crescent which brightened her whole face, and I couldn't help but smile back.

"This is my granddaughter, Serenity Dawn." A gray-haired lady with a kind voice placed her hands on Serenity's shoulders.

We talked for several minutes and I learned that Serenity Dawn and her grandparents were on their way to lead a weekly Bible study at a local nursing home. Her grandfather was a retired minister and every week the three of them volunteered at two different nursing homes in the city.

"Why don't you come?" Serenity's grandfather asked.

Feeling discouraged with my writing and more than a little curious, I grabbed my camera and notebook and followed them.

Nothing could have prepared me for what happened next.

The brightly lit activities center was packed with residents in wheelchairs crammed arm-to-arm. As her grandfather stood behind the podium reading from Scripture, Serenity Dawn, one of God's tiniest ministers, sat beside him on her grandmother's lap, with her pink romper and halo of golden curls, bearing witness to the Lord with her radiant smile.

After the service, Serenity followed her grandparents' lead and stopped by every resident's wheelchair, lacing her fingers in theirs and smiling with each one.

Suddenly, Serenity walked over to an empty place between two wheelchairs. She looked 'round and 'round and finally came back to her grandmother's side, a quizzical expression on her face.

"Serenity," her grandmother said in a soft voice, "your friend has gone home to be with Jesus." Serenity nodded. She understood.

And suddenly, I understood too.

I never finished the article I was writing that day. In fact, I can't even remember what it was about. All I know is that in her simple gesture of love, Serenity Dawn gave me a blessing more precious than words. I started writing from my heart—inspirational stories about people who touched my life and, suddenly, my words started connecting. It took a child, God's little messenger, to bless me in an unexpected way.

❧ Reflections

IF GOD WANTS US TO DO SOMETHING, then nothing, *absolutely nothing*, will be able to stop His creativity and ability within us. That's the lesson Maria learned in her encounter with Serenity Dawn. God had called her to write. She thought she couldn't succeed. But God provided the inspiration and freedom to fulfill His calling. The only thing that will prevent His productivity through us is our own failure to respond. If we cooperate, He will give us the time, energy, and passion to complete His will.

Is there an area in your life that you feel God's calling but doubt He can fulfill it through you? Have no fear. He will do it. All you have to do is cooperate.

Journal

Journal

But thanks be to God, who always leads us in triumphal procession in Christ and through us spreads everywhere the fragrance of the knowledge of him.

II CORINTHIANS 2:14

![] Unexpected Praise

Zig Ziglar

After I had been in the cookware business for a period of time, I realized I needed some help. I ran an ad in the Columbia, South Carolina, newspaper, and a woman named Gerry Arrowood responded. Prior to our interview, Gerry's work experience included baking cakes and taking in sewing to earn money for her family. The interview went quite well. She was quiet but pleasant. She explained to me when the interview was over that the job certainly sounded interesting and that she loved to cook. She even assured me that she did not mind washing dishes or cleaning the kitchen; however, she was shy and did not relate to people. Therefore, I must never call on her to participate in the demonstration. As she put it, "Zig, I'll do all the work—you do all the talking."

I could immediately tell that Gerry and I were going to get along real well—and we did for the next three months. Then one night my mouth overloaded my back, and I made more promises than time would let me keep. As a salesman in the cookware business, I conducted dinner demonstrations where we prepared meals for six or eight couples whom the hostess had invited into her home. The demonstrations enabled us to sell cookware to the hostess and guests. We then delivered the cookware to the purchasers and taught them how to use it on their own stoves.

I made too many appointments. When I realized I would be unable to keep them, I asked Gerry to help. She naturally asked about what I wanted her to do. I explained I wanted her to deliver the cookware to the six couples I had sold to that evening and teach them how to use it on their own stoves.

Terror appeared in Gerry's eyes. Her hands shook as she said, "I can't do it! I can't do it!"

I could not persuade her to change her mind. But on the way home, she gave it some more thought, and as she started to get out of the car, she said to me, "Okay, I'll do it. You stuck your neck out, and I don't want to see it cut off. However, let me be honest, Zig, and tell you that I won't sleep a wink tonight; I'll be absolutely miserable."

The next night I got one of the most exciting telephone calls I've ever received. Gerry was wound up tighter than a nine-day clock. With enormous enthusiasm, she said, "Zig, you cannot believe how much fun I've had today! The first family I delivered cookware to had the coffeepot on and a piece of cake waiting for me. They really bragged on me and told me how professional I was, what a nice personality I had, and how much they enjoyed having me in their home. They even invited me to come back with my girls and have dinner and said they would do the cooking! Three of the six couples had the coffee and dessert ready, and all of them told me what a good job I had done. They really made me feel good!"

She concluded our phone conversation by saying, "I don't ever remember having this much fun or feeling so good about myself. I'll be glad to do this for you anytime you want me to!" Her picture had just undergone a dramatic change.

It didn't happen that week, that month, or that year, but less than five years later, Gerry Arrowood was the international vice president in charge of sales training for a multimillion-dollar cosmetics company. I had no idea what an exciting future she had when I asked Gerry Arrowood to deliver those six sets of cookware.

How I wish I had retained the names of the customers Gerry met with that day, especially the first one. I have an idea that after the warm reception the first couple gave her, Gerry headed for that second home with considerably more excitement, enthusiasm, and confidence. That first couple turned out to be catalysts, didn't they? By seeing Gerry's good qualities and telling her about them, they started a growth process for Gerry that continues to this day.

Today, she and her husband, Bob Volberding, live in San Rafael, California, where they manufacture cosmetics for a number of private label, quality-conscious cosmetics companies. When the picture Gerry Arrowood had of herself changed, her life changed.

❧ *Reflections*

GERRY HAD A VISION PROBLEM . . . of herself. Zig opened the door of opportunity, but she had to walk through the door. Gerry only intended to walk through it one step and then run away again. When we're given a similar opening, you and I may back up. We're not sure God's blessings will greet us if we step through to the other side.

But with God on our side, we can't lose! He is in control. If we obey His leading, nothing can stop us or hinder us or slow us down. But we must take those agonizing steps. If we do, God promises blessings we could never imagine. Just ask Gerry. She'll tell you.

What's been holding you back from risking in obedience to God? It's really not a risk if God is in it.

Journal

_____

_____

_____

_____

_____

_____

_____

_____

_____

_____

_____

_____

_____

_____

_____

_____

_____

_____

_____

_____

_____

✍ Journal

_____
_____
_____
_____
_____
_____
_____
_____
_____
_____
_____
_____
_____
_____
_____
_____
_____
_____
_____
_____
_____
_____
_____
_____

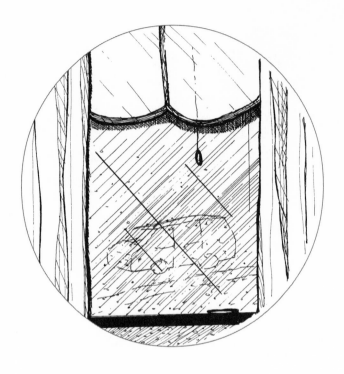

If you are willing and obedient, you will eat the best from the land.

ISAIAH 1:19

Depending On God

Laura Chalk

WE MARRIED THE SUMMER before my senior year of college. My husband, Jeff, five years older than me, was already in the work force. We decided I would finish school, get a job, and work for at least five years. Then we would start a family. We bought a house with a graduated loan. The monthly payments would be lower in the beginning, then, by the time I also had a job, we would be able to afford it. The plan sounded good to us.

But that was the problem: it was ours, not God's. Just nine months after we married, we were surprised to discover I was pregnant. We welcomed the news with great joy, but realized the plans we had made would need reevaluating. I would give birth to our son just months after graduation. Should I really start a career then?

Both of us became sensitive to the gentle whisper of God, who we believed didn't want me to work outside the home while we had young children. It wouldn't be easy. But we felt that if this was something God wanted us to do, He would take care of us.

On a cold, New Year's Day, our son was born. What a delicious feeling, to hold God's little blessing in my arms. My husband and I instantly fell in love with this precious gift. We looked at one another and knew. God's plans are much greater than ours could ever be.

Months passed, and we were enjoying our beautiful, thriving, little boy. I was so thankful we had followed God's lead. But we began to feel the pinch. The monthly payments on our mortgage were beginning to increase. How would we be able to afford our house if I wasn't contributing financially? We had to refinance our home, with a non-graduated payment schedule. It was a good time to refinance, as the interest rate had dropped, but we still didn't have the money to do it.

Days later, I was home playing with our son. The spring sky grew dark and ominous. Large, furious, hail hit quickly and with great force. I went to our front window to watch it pummel my tulips, and to my dismay, I saw that I had left the car in the driveway. I ran to the garage, opened the door, and stopped just short of stepping out into the hail. I knew I could be seriously hurt if I ventured out. I stood there, feeling helpless.

In a few minutes, the hail passed, but the car was richly texturized. After calling the insurance company, an adjuster came out the next day. Within a couple of weeks, we received a check in the mail from the insurance company. When we opened the envelope, we rejoiced with laughter and thanksgiving. The reimbursement for the car damage was the exact amount we needed to refinance the house. Years after, we enjoyed driving around in our permanently dimpled car, sharing the story of God's goodness with our friends.

Since that time, there have been other occasions God has stepped in at just the right time. Of course, we need to be financially responsible, but it's reassuring to know we're not in this alone. My husband and I have learned that as long as we are living in God's will for our lives, He will be with us every step of the way. Because we are obedient to Him, He continues to bless our family—even through unexpected hail.

❦ Reflections

"WHO WOULD HAVE EVER THOUGHT that God would use a hail storm to meet Laura and her families' need." Yet we can learn from her experience that when we completely give ourselves over to God's will and obey Him, He blesses us. He promises to take care of us—it just may not be in the way we imagined.

But isn't that the exciting thing about serving such a creative God? You never know what God has up His sleeve. Sometimes, it's a challenge to trust a God who surprises us. But if we continue to trust and depend on Him, we'll become more comfortable with His creativity and our faith will grow.

Has there been a time when you were disappointed in the way God unexpectedly answered a prayer? Try to look at the situation in a new way. You may find that it has more unexpected blessings than you originally thought.

Journal

Journal

In a large house there are articles not only of gold and silver, but also of wood and clay; some are for noble purposes and some for ignoble. If a man cleanses himself from the latter, he will be an instrument for noble purposes, made holy, useful to the Master and prepared to do any good work.

II Timothy 2:20, 21

![] The Noble Spork

Joni Eareckson Tada

I WAS HAVING LUNCH at a friend's home recently, a wise Christian woman with discerning eyes. Before we ate, I had to borrow one of her spoons and have her bend and twist it in a contorted angle.

She then inserted the spoon in my hand splint and I was able to feed myself. But as we ate and casually talked, I noticed her eyes. She kept looking at the bent spoon. When lunch was over she pulled the spoon out of my arm splint, and set it by my plate. I was a little embarrassed that I had to bend one of her nicest pieces of flatware. With that ugly twist of the metal, it looked as though I had ruined the spoon.

I offered to have my husband straighten out the spoon—to return it to its original shape.

"Oh, no," she said. "I want to keep this spoon just the way it is."

"But it looks ugly like that," I protested, "and besides, you won't be able to use it." By this time she had the spoon in her hand, gently fingering the twist in the handle, admiring it as though it were a thing of beauty rather than something bent and misshapen. To her, the spoon had a special meaning.

"You see, Joni," she explained, "you can only use a spoon that's been bent to meet your needs. A straight one just won't do. A twisted tool in your hand can better accomplish a task."

I've nicknamed my special utensil a "spork." I can't tell you how many times I've gone into a restaurant and had busboys or a waitress spy it and try to take it away.

"Ugh! Where did this come from? It must have gotten mangled in the dishwasher," they'll say.

Or a busboy may pick it up and without saying a word, bend it back to its original shape, thinking he's doing me a favor.

"Oh no," I tell them. "It's supposed to look like that. It's bent perfectly so I can use it."

Isn't that the way God works in our lives? He knows He can better accomplish His unique plan when He bends us to suit His will. He can best use us when we're molded and shaped for His special design. Now, certainly, this spork of mine isn't very attractive. It's obviously unlike the rest of the utensils in the kitchen drawer. And we might come to think that we, in our weakness, are unlike all the rest.

But in the hand of God we serve an express purpose. The metal of our souls may be hard and difficult to bend, but when we allow God the privilege of shaping our lives, we discover new depths of purpose and meaning. What a joyful thought to realize you are a chosen vessel for God—perfectly suited for His use.

Even a spork can be noble . . . if it's placed in the Master's hand.

❧ Reflections

HOW WE LONG TO BE A USEFUL VESSEL in the
Master's hand. His gentle touch will mold us into a noble instrument that will bring blessings untold. There is nothing more
fulfilling than to be used by Him. Joni has experienced that, just
like her noble spork. Certainly, Joni's paralysis seemed too difficult for God to bring good. But God had a more noble purpose.

In the same way, trials, temptations, and disease may assail us
and we groan in disappointment. How can God use us in such
pain? Just like Joni's spork, we may be fashioned in such a way
that we appear unuseable. Yet, God is carving us into a servant
that can be compatible with His special plan for us. If we'll just
bend with His tender touch, we'll experience blessings we never
anticipated.

How have you seen God use His "bending" of you in
the past? In what ways was it an unexpected blessing?
Can you see potential blessings from His current
molding of you?

~§ Journal

Journal

Though you have made me see troubles, many and bitter, you will restore my life again; from the depths of the earth you will again bring me up.

PSALM 71:20

An Encounter With A Stranger

Pauline Jaramillo

I SCANNED THE CROWDED AIRPORT LOBBY, saw a row of empty seats at the back of the room, and began to move toward them. I paused to let a group of people walk by and noticed a lady sitting immediately to my right surrounded by several empty seats. Her upper body, legs and arms were moving rhythmically. I looked away and took a step forward, then changed my mind and sat next to her. After a brief silence and perpetual motion, she introduced herself and in the same breath said, "I have Parkinson's Disease."

"I'm majoring in Rehabilitation Counseling," I responded, "if you would like to share your personal experience with the disease, I would like to hear it."

She sighed, "I can't wait to get back home. I don't like traveling." She looked down then lifted her head and looked at me. There was a brief silence while she seemed to struggle with a decision. "Ten years ago I was diagnosed with this disease," she began, "since then I've attempted suicide twice. I'm sure I'll succeed the next time."

Her statement took me by surprise. I was expecting information that would be helpful to me, instead I found myself struggling with the weight of her burden. She proceeded to describe her despair; each statement was punctuated by the lunging and swaying of her body. As she continued speaking, half of my mind listened and the other half considered and discarded counseling techniques which I had learned in class. None of them seemed appropriate. "Lord, tell me what to say," I prayed silently.

When she paused, I shared briefly my personal struggle with hurt, anger, and fear as a result of living with an alcoholic father, and what had brought me through it. She listened closely as I described how God had lead me to key verses in the Scriptures.

"Do you have a Bible at home?" I asked.

"Yes, but I don't read it much."

I took a notebook from my purse and wrote down some Scripture references. "If you promise to read these, I promise to pray for you daily." She smiled, took the sheet of paper and said, "Thank you for sitting next to me. Most people avoid me."

Before I could respond, a voice over the intercom announced that our flight was cleared for boarding. We were separated in the crowd of people and sat in different locations. As we waited for takeoff, I looked out the window and contemplated God's perfect timing. While I was scanning the lobby hoping to find a quiet place to sit, He had planned an encounter with a stranger and an unexpected blessing.

❧ *Reflections*

PAULINE'S WILLINGNESS to be sensitive to the needs of a hurting woman brought an opportunity to see God work. We may not always know the wounded souls that sit around us in an airport, buy groceries beside us in a store, or even sit beside us in our church pew. But if we will be sensitive to the leading of God's Holy Spirit, we can cooperate with His perfect timing—and receive an unexpected blessing of being able to make a difference in someone's life.

Will you make a fresh commitment to use your spiritual antenna to be sensitive to God's leading? You'll have the joy of experiencing an unexpected blessing.

✒ Journal

Journal

*Hope deferred makes the heart sick, but a
longing fulfilled is a tree of life.*

Proverbs 13:12

My Best Friend

Karen Kosman

ONE MORNING THIS SUMMER, a staccato of laughter rang out from our front yard. As I stood and watched, my husband ran around a tree with two preschool tots close behind. My heart beat with joy. Suddenly, he stopped and turned, scooping both children up. They screamed and wiggled to get free, until he sat down. Then Lauren, age four (a curly headed cherub), and Kenny, age five (mischievous from head to toe), both looked at their granddad with a look that stated, "I love you."

As I walked over to the fence I thought how God had blessed me with a second chance—to have a Christian husband.

At age sixty-three, John stands five foot eight. His bronze complexion is a pleasant contrast to the crown of curly, silver hair. Almond shaped hazel eyes, full of merriment, embrace life through dark-brown rimmed glasses. Devoted to weekly work-outs, his physique is firm, except for "the battle of the bulge or the middle-aged spread" that began three years ago with retirement.

These past fourteen years have been so richly blessed. As a blended family we have seven adult children, and thirteen grand-children. There has been a mixture of joy and tears.

Reflecting on the past, I remember as a single Mom how life didn't leave much room for a social life. I had been single for seven years and had stopped trying to find someone. My friends teased me, "Karen, when are you going to find Mr. Right and get married again?"

I answered, "When I meet a man with six kids." I didn't think I'd ever meet a man with six kids so I concluded I was safe in making such a ridiculous statement.

I met John at a Christian singles fellowship. As we became acquainted, I asked, "How many children do you have, John?

"Six."

"Excuse me?"

"I have six children. The youngest is sixteen."

Stifling a laugh, I looked up at the sky and whispered. "Oh no!" The unexpected happened—I met a man with six kids. If you can't beat them, join them. One year later John and I were married.

John has many attributes that are endearing. He is sensitive, witty, compassionate, a devoted husband, dad, and grandfather. He declares, "I love to make people laugh."

Both John and I had lost hope when divorce had turned life upside down. Our broken hearts were shattered, but God's mercy and love became a tree of life and he blessed us with a second chance. In Christ we have become whole. I'm so proud of John when he openly shares with others how God has taken jealousy, alcoholism, and panic attacks out of his life.

John looked up from playing with Lauren and Kenny. He walked over to the fence, kissed me, and smiled as he said, "I love you more today than yesterday."

Tell me, am I blessed?

✍ Reflections

AFTER EXPERIENCING THE GRIEF of being widowed or divorced, many people, even those trusting God, believe that they can no longer experience any happiness. Their hurt and loneliness find it hard to believe that God might unexpectedly bless them with a loving relationship. Yet Karen's story proves that God can do something beyond our ability to imagine. He knows how He wants to meet the needs of each individual, whether through continued singleness or marriage. He is weaving in each of our lives a cloth of many colors to bring Him glory. If your cloth seems a little threadbare right now, maybe He has a surprise planned of adding new threads.

Are you lonely or hurting, either as a single person or in your marriage? Don't give up hope. With God, there is always the possibility of a new thread being added to your life.

Journal

Journal

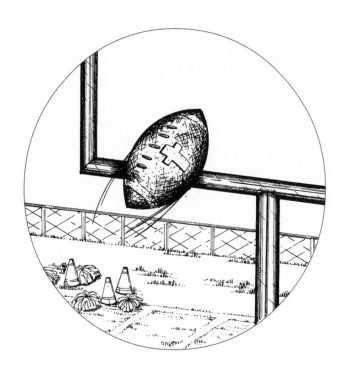

We are therefore Christ's ambassadors, as though God were making his appeal through us. We implore you on Christ's behalf: Be reconciled to God.

II CORINTHIANS 5:20

A Chance Meeting That Wasn't By "Chance"

Bob Turnbull

IT WAS A SUNDAY AFTERNOON when I drove to the post office to pick up our box mail. As I drove into the parking lot there was only one other car there. I parked two slots away. As I got out of the car I was aware there was a couple in the car arguing.

As I walked through the doors, I heard a male voice shouting from the car, "Coach?" As I turned around, the man got out of his car. I recognized him as one of my players when I coached high school football. I'll call him Brad. I hadn't seen him for ten years.

He walked in with me and started talking.

"Coach, my wife and I are at a crossroads. You obviously know I'm black and she's white. That has never been a problem for either one of us, when we were dating or in our marriage. Never. Unfortunately, it has been a problem with both sides of our families, especially mine. We usually get along fine, but we're now nit-picking at each other over trivial matters. It's starting to affect our kids. I need some of your good counsel."

"I appreciate that, Brad," I replied, "but why aren't you receiving counsel from our Lord? Or is He not an active part of your life and your marriage now?"

He hung his head and said, "You nailed it coach."

"Coach, over the years, I started slowly sliding away from God and pretty soon He was out of the picture entirely."

At the same time Brad took a breath, his wife, tired of waiting in the car, walked in. He quickly introduced her to me, and her face went from a frown to a smile. "Oh, hi, coach. Good to meet you. I've heard so much about you over the years from Brad."

I asked Jenny where she thought her spiritual life was at this time. Her honest answer was, "I don't really have one, but I know I should. I feel incomplete, like something is missing. Brad and I used to talk about this but neither of us does nowadays." Then I was pleasantly surprised yet thankful to hear her say, "Will you help us find a spiritual life together?"

I glanced over to Brad and he was beaming. We grabbed hands and the three of us had the most open, loving and free-flowing talk on Christ becoming real in their lives. About one hour later, with the post office still empty, Jenny bowed her head, and with her tears unashamedly flowing, she prayed and asked Jesus to come into her heart. With tears in his eyes, Brad rededicated his life to Christ and promised Him that he would be the spiritual leader of his home.

As we were all departing, Brad looked at me and said, "Coach, what a coincidence to bump into you here in the post office after ten years. We don't even live in this area anymore but were just down to visit her mom. At the last moment I zipped in here to mail some of our bills."

He heard what he was saying and quickly said, "Whoops, I forgot. You don't believe in coincidence when God is involved with one of His children, do you?"

"Good recall, Brad. You're right. I don't. For me to come to the post office at the same time you zipped in to mail a letter, well, that is what you call a chance meeting that isn't by 'chance'."

❧ Reflections

WE DON'T ALWAYS SEE THE FRUIT that God brings from the seeds that we plant in people's lives. Bob was given a glimpse of how his earlier contact in a high school setting would later make a difference in a couple's life—in an unexpected "chance meeting." Of course, we know that God orchestrates everything in our lives and there are no "coincidences." It's a thrill to see God move in such an obvious way and thus build our faith. We know that nothing said or done in Jesus' name is wasted. Most of the time, it won't be until we're in heaven that we'll receive the unexpected blessing of seeing how our lives touched others.

❧

Are you discouraged because it seems like your efforts aren't bearing fruit in the lives of others? Trust that God is using you more than your human sight can see.

Journal

❧ Journal

Let your conversation be always full of grace,
seasoned with salt, so that you may know
how to answer everyone.

COLOSSIANS 4:18

The Blessing Of Communication

Jan Woodard

MY FRIEND SANDY and I walked the high school track one summer evening. As we exercised, we discussed stressors newlyweds face adjusting to the realities of married life.

"When Jim and I married as college seniors, we thought we understood all there was to know about love and life," I laughed, "but we soon discovered we had different ideas on almost everything—like hamburgers. I liked 'em fat, he liked 'em flat."

As my friend and I rounded a curve, I told her of one spring morning that first year when I fixed a simple breakfast for two on the backyard patio of the house we rented.

"How romantic," I thought as I wiped dew from the white wrought iron chairs and table. "Just the two of us, beginning our day together outdoors before classes."

When Jim stepped out ten minutes later, he looked at the table and said in a practical voice, "Never pour milk on my cereal; now it's soggy."

All the romance of the moment was doused by his words and I marched away in a huff. But still, as he requested, I've never poured milk on his cereal again.

Then Sandy said something I never thought about before. "At least you both were able to express your opinions. My husband never expressed his ideas about anything, so I assumed he agreed with mine. I was shocked when he moved out twelve years later; I didn't even know our marriage was in trouble. Maybe if he'd told me what he thought all along, we could have worked things out."

At her words, I shivered in the early evening air. I know it's only through God's grace that my husband and I have learned the high cost of committed love, slowly laying down our own self-centered ways, wills and wants, and replacing them with more Christ-centered and other-centered attitudes.

And I'm still learning. I can see now, through Sandy's sad comment, that what I've sometimes considered to be a negative—two people expressing strong ideas and firm convictions about the little details of daily life—is actually an unexpected blessing. Perhaps Jim and I have a strong marriage today not only because of the happy memories we've built together, but also because of the communication struggles we've faced and overcome. Marriage, like muscles, grows stronger with resistance and exercise.

❧ Reflections

SOMEONE HAS SAID love isn't made up of big stuff nearly as much as it is of a series of small daily sacrifices. It's passing along little blessings that keeps a marriage, or any relationship, healthy: fixing the coffee when you're in a rush and don't feel like washing the pot; listening with a sympathetic ear when you'd rather watch Tom Brokaw; offering to pick up the kids at midnight from a school trip so your spouse can get extra sleep. Learning to love is a lifelong process. As Jan learned, dying to self is one of the hardest things in the world. Yet when we make that difficult choice, we see God's unexpected blessings.

Do you need to recognize and confess to God any impatience, unkindness, or pride? Who will be unexpectedly blessed by your intentional, supportive acceptance of her or him today? Try it, you'll like it.

Journal

Journal

"For who has known the mind of the Lord that he may instruct him?" But we have the mind of Christ.

I CORINTHIANS 2:16

The Deal Of A Lifetime

Charles Stanley

WHEN I WAS FIRST STARTING OUT in the ministry, a businessman offered me an opportunity to invest in his company. He assured me it was a very low-risk investment. He knew I didn't have much money, and it was his way of helping me out. I didn't have any reason to doubt his sincerity so I took the paperwork home to my wife, Anna, and we read it together.

At first, neither one of us had any reservations. But a couple of days later I was in my study praying about something else, and suddenly, the business venture popped into my mind. I immediately had an uneasy feeling about the whole thing. From then on, anytime I thought or prayed about it, I had misgivings. When I would try to argue the point, my conscience would bother me. I knew that the moment I gave him a check, I would feel guilty. I could feel the guilt beforehand.

Anna had the same premonition. When she shared how she felt, that settled it for me. We thanked the gentleman for his interest and politely declined his offer. Years later we heard through the grapevine that he was forced to declare bankruptcy. Everybody who had invested with him lost the entire investment.

All of us will be given opportunities to participate in things that are not God's will. They are not necessarily bad things. They just aren't God's best for us at the time. If not for the work of the Holy Spirit in our lives, we would have no way of knowing. That is why it is so important to develop sensitivity to the

Holy Spirit. We must go beyond evaluating things based on their moral or ethical merit alone. There is more to decision making for the child of God than that. We must allow the Spirit-filled conscience to discern. Only then can we know what is and what is not of God.

Reflections

THOSE WHO SEEK GOD'S WISDOM are truly the most blessed, as Charles' example proves. We have available to us the very mind of Christ, able to be guided with the vast knowledge of God Himself. No, we won't always know everything and we are bound to make mistakes—even when we think we're doing the right thing. But God offers us the blessed advantage of discernment that far surpasses human knowledge. We are truly blessed. God's very Spirit resides in us! When we want to avoid unexpected failure and disappointment, we only need to seek Him and obey. Then, we'll receive unexpected blessings.

Are you facing a decision? Does your mind seem cloudy and confused? Ask God for His discerning mind. It is available as part of your inheritance in Christ.

Journal

Journal

Trust in the LORD with all your heart and
lean not on your own understanding; in all
your ways acknowledge him and he will
make your paths straight.

PROVERBS 3:5, 6

God Had
Another Plan

Diana L. James

THE HOUSE LIGHTS DIMMED. A hush fell over the audience. Beyond the glare of the spotlight, six hundred eyes focused on the person in the center of the stage—me.

Perspiration trickled down my cheek and along the side of my neck. I smiled, then leaned toward the microphone to welcome the audience. But the sounds I made bore little resemblance to my normal speaking voice. It was as if the batteries on a tape player had run down, turning my voice into a guttural, s-l-o-w—m-o-t-i-o-n growl.

Although the audience may have interpreted it as the typical stage fright of a beginner speaker, that wasn't the case. For years, I had spoken for large audiences, hosted my own TV program, and had just been accurately introduced as a professional speaker.

So what was happening? That question jabbed my mind while I fought to regain control of my body and live up to the glowing introduction I had just received. It was like a nightmare when you need to run but can't because your legs seem encased in cement.

Silently, I said, "Get a grip. You've done this hundreds of times. Oh, please God, I need Your help."

God must have sent an angel, because I got through the speech—with warm applause at the end. But I knew something was terribly wrong. I was bathed in perspiration; my hands were shaking, and I was sure my voice had sounded like Kermit the Frog with a bad case of the flu.

A physical exam revealed Graves Disease—not a minor problem, but a severe form of hyperactive thyroid, hard to cure, and usually progressive. I asked God, "Why would You do this to me, just when my speaking career was surging toward success? Lord, why is this happening?"

God didn't answer and my symptoms got worse. In addition to my now quirky voice and body thermostat, my "do it now" modus operandi was replaced by debilitating fatigue.

I had no choice. I canceled my speaking engagements, stopped calling meeting planners, and quit my membership in the National Speakers Association. Resentment wove a paralyzing grip through my thinking—until one day, when a small plaque that had sat on my desk for seven years suddenly came to life.

I knew the words on it by heart, but, that day, the words jumped down off that plaque, leapt into my heart, and became a part of me forever. *Trust in the LORD and lean not on your own understanding. In all your ways acknowledge Him and He will direct your path* (Proverbs 3:5, 6).

In that instant, I knew it didn't matter if my speaking career was gone. I felt complete trust in the Lord. Acknowledging Him as Lord of my life, I felt at peace. Sensing His guidance, I started writing nonfiction articles which were published in national magazines. I wrote and illustrated a children's book for my seven-year-old grandson. I compiled stories about how people "bounced back" from traumas and troubles.

This thrill had an extra dimension because my mother, who made her living as a writer, had always wanted to write a book and never got the chance.

"This one's for you, Momma," I said through happy tears when the book contract arrived. I could almost see Momma up in Heaven, cheering and clapping her hands.

The book, *Bounce Back*, is now a reality. My Graves Disease appears to be cured, and I'm speaking to audiences again. When I put my trust in God, He took what appeared to be bad, and turned it into a blessing. The book, which might never have been written if I hadn't become ill, is now blessing hundreds of people with it's message of hope. Thanks be to God for His unexpected, but welcomed plan.

❧ *Reflections*

WHEN WE'RE IN A PIT OF UNCERTAINTY, especially an illness that may not be curable, it's easy to think God doesn't have a plan at all, much less a positive result. Yet, we are reminded through Diana's story that God does know the plan He has for each of us. As we trust in Him we will see blessings we never could have created ourselves. At the time of our distress, we may be tempted to give in to despair. If Diana had done that, she never would have become an author or have her speaking ministry expanded and blessed. God wants us to patiently hold on and "bounce back" so that He can give us the full measure of His blessings.

❧

Is a difficulty plaguing you and causing you to feel like God has given up on you? Hang in there and "bounce back." God's unexpected blessing will find you.

Journal

❧ Journal

So do not worry, saying, "what shall we eat?" or "What shall we drink?" or "What shall we wear?" For the pagans run after all these things, and your heavenly Father knows that you need them. But seek first his kingdom and his righteousness, and all these things will be given to you as well.

MATTHEW 6:31–33

Unexpected Dinner

Penelope Carlevato

W E HAD ONE GOAL IN OUR LIVES as a young couple: get rich quick. We had become involved in a pyramid business and nearly lost everything we had. This experience, however, had an unexpected, life changing result, as we found new life and new goals when we became Christians.

The months that followed were probably the most exciting times of our lives, as we walked by faith for all our needs, and sought to get back on our feet financially.

To help out, I began baby-sitting for a little two-year-old boy in our neighborhood. Jeffrey and our three children had a great time playing together. His mother was a flight attendant and liked our life style. She felt comfortable leaving her little guy with us, and we loved him.

One afternoon I realized we had no food and no money for dinner. At first I panicked, but then remembered Matthew 6:31-33 that I had read in my Bible that morning. It told me to not be anxious, but instead seek His kingdom first. Okay, Lord, I will trust you.

I thought my husband would come home with a "miracle," but he entered the front door about 6:00 p.m. empty handed. I shared with him my concern and we both prayed about what we should do. I rechecked the refrigerator and the kitchen cabinets to make sure I hadn't overlooked something.

About that time, Jeffrey's mother arrived to take him home, her arms loaded with bags. "Surprise!" she exclaimed, "You don't have to cook tonight! The flight I just arrived on had an unusually large number of leftover dinners from First Class, and they were going to throw all this food away. There is enough food for all of us."

That evening, as we dined on First Class dinners, we thanked the Lord for His blessing that He provided in an unexpected way.

❧ Reflections

MOST OF US WON'T FLY FIRST CLASS, much less have First Class dinners delivered to our homes. Yet Penelope's story proves that God is interested in every part of our lives. If we will seek Him, everything we need will be provided—although maybe not in such an amusing way. Whether or not it is, God wants us to depend upon Him and see His provision build our dependence upon Him. Nothing is too difficult for God and none of our needs is too small for Him to take care of.

Are you feeling anxious, worried that God will not provide one of your needs? If you seek Him and His righteousness, He promises to meet all your true needs.

❧ Journal

_____
_____
_____
_____
_____
_____
_____
_____
_____
_____
_____
_____
_____
_____
_____
_____
_____
_____
_____

✍ Journal

. . . give thanks in all circumstances, for this is God's will for you in Christ Jesus.

I THESSALONIANS 5:18

Unexpected Gratitude

Max Lucado

I HAD EVERY RIGHT TO BE ANGRY.

My problems began on Sunday night. I was still in Brazil and was taking some relatives to southern Brazil to see the Iguacu Falls. A canceled flight left us stranded several hours in the Sao Paulo airport. No warning. No explanation. Just a notification as we were landing that the plane we were going to catch was going nowhere. If we wanted, we could wait two hours and catch another one.

"If we wanted!" Grrrr.

When we got to our hotel, it was raining. It rained until the day we left.

When I got back to the hotel, I realized that the rain had ruined the recorder. How much ruin? Three hundred dollars' worth of ruin. That was Wednesday. The week wasn't over yet.

Thursday was the clincher. Denalyn called me at home. Our car had broken down. The car that the car dealer promised was in great shape. Downtown. Again. On my day off.

I sat in the car and tried to start it. No luck. When I turned the key in the ignition all I could hear were the promises of the car dealer and the jingle of the mechanic's cash register. I spent an hour tinkering with a broken-down car in a parking lot.

Finally I called the mechanic. The tow truck was busy. Could I wait a few minutes? In Brazil, the word minutes can better be translated "years." So I waited. And I waited. And I waited. My children grew up and had children of their own and still I was waiting.

Finally, as the sun was setting, the truck appeared. "Put it in neutral," I was instructed. As I climbed in the car I thought, *Might as well try it one more time.* I turned the key in the ignition. Guess what? You got it. It started.

That should be good news. It was, until I saw the driver of the tow truck in no hurry to leave. He wanted to be paid. "For what?" I implored. "Was it my fault your car started?" he replied. It's a good thing I didn't know how to say "smart aleck" in Portuguese. So I paid him for watching me start my car.

I immediately drove the car to the mechanic. As I drove, two devils came and perched on my shoulders. They spoke the language of the Liar.

One was anger. My list of offenses was long and ugly.

The other was self-pity. Not only had I had a bad week, he reminded me that I had been plagued with a bad life! Born with the handicap of freckles and red hair. And now, a missionary suffering on foreign soil.

Anger in one ear and self-pity in the other . . . if I hadn't seen him, who knows what I would have done.

He didn't look like an angel. But I know he was an angel, for only angels bring that type of a message.

He knocked on my car window.

"Trocadinho, Senhor?" ("Do you have any spare change, sir?")

He was, at most, nine years old. Shirtless. Barefoot. Dirty. So dirty, I couldn't tell if he was wearing shorts or not. His hair was matted. His skin was crusty. I rolled down the window. The voices on my shoulders became silent.

"What's your name?" I asked.

"Jose."

I looked over at the sidewalk. Two other street orphans were walking towards the cars behind me. They were naked except for ragged gym shorts.

"Are they your brothers?" I asked.

"No, just friends."

"Have you collected much money today?"

He opened a dirty hand full of coins. Enough money, perhaps, for a soft drink.

I reached in my wallet and pulled out the equivalent to a dollar. His eyes brightened. Mine watered. As I drove away I saw him running to tell his friends what he had received.

The voices on my shoulders didn't dare say a word. Nor did I. The three of us drove in shameful silence.

What if God had responded to my grumblings? He could have answered my carelessly mumbled prayers. And had he chosen to do so, a prototype of the result had just appeared at my door.

"Don't want to mess with airlines? This boy doesn't have that problem. Frustrated with your VCR? That's one headache this boy doesn't have. He may have to worry about tonight's dinner, but he doesn't have to worry about VCRs. And family? I'm sure this orphan would gladly take one of your families if you are too busy to appreciate them. And cars? Yes, they are a hassle, aren't they? You should try this boy's mode of transportation—bare feet."

Jose gave me a lot for my dollar; he gave me a lesson on gratitude.

Reflections

WE NEVER KNOW HOW MUCH we are blessed until we see the misfortune of others. Max received an unexpected jolt of gratitude through the lesson of a beggar. What does God have to unexpectedly bring into our lives to develop our attitudes of gratitude? Let's not give Him the opportunity—or the necessity. We have an excess of things and relationships. We can focus on them, instead of our imagined wants (though we call them "needs") in order to discover the great joy of a grateful heart. And if you need a jolt, just remember that nine-year-old boy who brightened at the thought of a dollar.

What have you been thinking you can't live without? Surrender it to the Lord. He'll provide it if you truly need it.

❧ Journal

❧ Journal

Journal

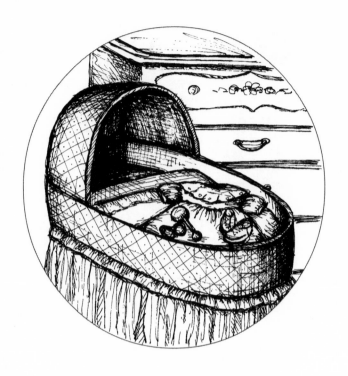

But as for me, I will always have hope;
I will praise you more and more.

PSALM 71:14

Dream A Little Dream

Rhonda Wheeler Stock

I LOVE MY BOYS. They delight my husband and me with their unending creativity and affectionate natures. They were—and are—kind and clever and generally well-behaved. I thank God for blessing us with three healthy sons; I count it a privilege to raise up warriors for the kingdom of God.

But deep in my heart, I longed for a daughter. I wanted someone to dress up and fuss over—boys tolerate only so much fussing. I wanted someone to whom I could teach the fine art of bargain hunting, someone to take with me to the hairdresser for an afternoon of beautifying. My husband also wanted a girl; he pictured a sweetheart who would always have a hug and a kiss for her Daddy. Even the boys thought it would be fun to have a sister.

We decided to adopt a baby girl. Before we had even met, my husband and I each wanted to adopt a child someday. Not because we were socially conscious superheroes, but because it somehow seemed right. After we married, we discovered this dream we shared. Someday, we promised ourselves, we'll do it.

We researched our options. Because we already had three children, it was unlikely we could adopt an American-born infant. We felt God directing us toward an international adoption anyway, and we didn't mind the thought of a slightly older child. Because of a miscarriage, we had a large gap between children; maybe this was God's way of filling that gap.

We chose a reputable Christian agency that specializes in international adoptions. We filled out forms, hired a social worker, filled out forms, went to the police station to be finger-printed, and filled out forms. We grumbled about the lengthy process but knew we had no choice.

The phone rang one cold January morning. It was our social worker who explained, "One of our agency's clients has given birth prematurely. The baby girl needs an immediate placement and your paperwork is ready to process. Would you consider changing your plans and take this child instead?"

Would we! Our choice seemed obvious, but we wanted to be sure we were being led by God and not by our own hopeful hearts. We prayed. We talked with the neonatal specialists, the hospital social worker, and our own social worker. We prayed. We carefully considered the baby's condition and future risks. We prayed. We asked, "What will be best for our family as well as for this tiny person?" And we prayed.

Finally, we knew what to do. We loved this baby regardless of the risks. In some supernatural way, God had already bonded our hearts to her. We were a family, and this child was part of us.

At the hospital, I clipped a tiny pink and white bow to a tuft of silky blond hair. As I held this incredibly fragile four-pound human being—my daughter—I thought of her other mother, the young woman who had given life to this child. That young woman could have paid a doctor to suction the life from her womb. Society would say she had every reason to do so; she was young, alone, and poor. Instead, she allowed her tragedy to become someone else's blessing.

I returned my sleeping angel to her Isolette and breathed a prayer of thanksgiving. "And, God, bless this baby's mother," I added, then I paused. "Bless both her mothers."

✑ Reflections

SOMETIMES GOD GIVES US A DREAM, then makes it
even better. Rhonda saw her dreams come true, but in a greater
measure than she ever expected. Isn't that just like our great
God? With a delighted smile on His face, He gives us an inner
desire and then fulfills it in His own unexpected way. We may
think He's going to do it in a certain way, but He knows all
along the plan He has in mind. And that plan will always be for
our good. Just ask Rhonda and that new baby daughter she's
holding in her arms.

Is there a God-given desire in your heart that hasn't
been fulfilled? Don't assume you know the complete
picture God has in mind. He might unexpectedly
surprise you.

✒ Journal

_____
_____
_____
_____
_____
_____
_____
_____
_____
_____
_____
_____
_____
_____
_____
_____
_____
_____
_____
_____
_____

❧ Journal

_____
_____
_____
_____
_____
_____
_____
_____
_____
_____
_____
_____
_____
_____
_____
_____
_____
_____
_____
_____
_____
_____

*Don't you know that you yourselves are
God's temple and that God's Spirit lives in
you? If anyone destroys God's temple, God
will destroy him; for God's temple is sacred,
and you are that temple.*

I Corinthians 3:16, 17

A Head 'n Heart Collision

Janice L. Krouskop

THE MAY SUNSHINE and clear blue sky did nothing to chase away the cloudy mood in the car as I drove Dad to his doctor's appointment. The gloomy silence confirmed what we both knew would soon be said . . .

"We can't wait any longer," said the doctor, "It's time. Your kidneys aren't working, you must begin hemodialysis." The emotion in her voice betrayed her feelings for us both. She was not only Dad's doctor but also my supervisor.

I was no stranger to dialysis. I worked as a registered dietitian in the outpatient hemodialysis clinic and was familiar with the routine treatments: typically three times a week for at least three hours which cleansed the blood, doing what the kidneys could no longer do. I knew about the needles, tubes, machines, dietary restrictions, and medications needed to keep dialysis patients alive. This was my professional world and it was about to collide with my personal life.

That afternoon I took Dad to the clinic for a tour. "Please, God," I prayed, "Let a perky patient be there so Dad won't be totally grossed out." In answer to prayer I spotted Henry, my favorite patient, leaving the clinic. In the middle of the sidewalk in the glow of the sunshine Henry reassured Dad about the lifeline of dialysis. "Thank you, Lord," I whispered to myself and stepped back so not to intrude on this very meaningful conversation.

Several weeks later, I felt the full impact of my professional-personal collision. Dad wasn't just a dialysis patient, he was my patient. Dad wasn't accustomed to taking instructions from me and I wasn't used to telling him he must give up foods he loved. Fluid restrictions were the hardest. Unfortunately, Dad was not following my professional advice and his lab values proved it. It was hurting his health and my heart. The doctor finally had a talk with Dad saying, "Do you think I would employ staff members who don't know what they are doing? Your daughter is giving you the best advice for your life. Listen to her."

Slowly, Dad complied with the medical instructions and dietary restrictions. His health improved enough to be evaluated for the transplant waiting list. I was so thankful but so very weary. The jolt of the collision between dietitian and daughter had jarred the protective detachment health care professionals need to survive. My personal empathy with patients and their families was causing professional burn out.

It was God's strong, loving arms that restored me. One day in prayer I heard Him gently say, "Jan, this experience is a blessing. Few people ever get a professional and personal perspective of chronic illness. This insight will give you the power and passion to inspire others to live well."

A Scripture verse came to mind, *Don't you know that you yourselves are God's temple and that God's spirit lives in you?* (I Corinthians 3:16). That day I knew my future was in wellness promotion rather than medical nutrition therapy. The clash of my personal and professional lives began to heal into a merciful merger of body, mind, and spirit, the three dimensions of wellness.

By his one year anniversary of beginning dialysis, Dad was medically stable and on the transplant waiting list. With a teary good-bye and a vision of wellness promotion, I resigned from my job at the clinic and began my journey into professional speaking. I now give presentations to both secular and Christian audiences on the art of living well in body, mind, and spirit. My purpose and passion were unexpectedly inspired by my two Dads: John Uncapher, my earthly Dad, and God, my Heavenly Father who lives in me.

Dad was blessed with a kidney transplant a year later in April, 1996. His new lease on life has inspired him to speak too. Dad gives talks to community groups sharing his experience and urging others to sign organ donor cards.

God is so good.

ᦰ Reflections

IT MIGHT HAVE BEEN EASY for Janice to ignore God's leading because of the conflict in her heart about her Dad's illness. When we are hurting, we are often blinded to God's work. While in the midst of caring for her Dad, Janice had no clue to the higher purpose God had in this situation. You and I often want to avoid pain and conflict, yet the Lord desires that a greater good be birthed from our involvement. A collision between our head and heart may just explode into an unexpected blessing.

Are you grumbling about God's plan because it's too painful to see someone you love suffer? The final chapter hasn't been written. Let God write it, don't write it yourself.

Journal

Journal

And without faith it is impossible to please
God, because anyone who comes to him must
believe that he exists and that he rewards those
who earnestly seek him.

HEBREWS 11:6

![] Unexpected Faith

Ruth Bell Graham

"Ruth," SAID AN OLD HIGH SCHOOL FRIEND who had been studying at a secular university, "you ought to lose your faith. It would do you good."

No one had ever suggested that to me before, and it took me completely by surprise. But the seed was planted and it began to bear fruit, slowly but relentlessly.

I cannot say that I became an atheist. It takes more faith to be an atheist than to believe in God. It was impossible for me to look at the heavens at night without realizing there had to be a Creator. But I could not be sure the Bible was God's message to man, and if I could not be sure of that, I could not be sure that Jesus was who He claimed to be.

I began to argue. I argued with anyone who was willing to argue.

It got to where people would avoid me when confrontation was inevitable.

"Here comes Ruth," was the general opinion of my friends, "we're in for another argument."

They didn't understand: I wasn't arguing to win, I was arguing desperately to lose. I wanted them to come up with valid reasons that I was wrong and they were right.

At that time, I had been dating a senior reputed to be one of the most brilliant students on campus. It didn't take him long to realize my predicament.

"You're having problems with your faith, aren't you?" he asked one day.

"You can say that again!" I replied.

"Let's go and see so-and-so," he suggested, naming a deeply spiritual professor on campus.

I objected.

"He will talk with me, and pray with me, and it could even get a little emotional. I don't want that. All I want are cold, hard facts." I wanted to go see Dr. Gordon Clark, known for his logic, his unemotional brilliance. I felt he would give me nothing but the cold, hard facts.

My friend wound up by explaining to me simply, factually, and logically why we believe the Bible is God's message to man, whom He had made—man, who had turned his back on God, for whom God felt responsible, and to whom God was reaching out.

I do not remember all the arguments. Today they seem unimportant. What I do remember is the final step. At the very end he said, "There is still the leap of faith." It was exactly what I needed: the clear, terse arguments, the merciless logic, and finally, the "leap of faith."

If God could be reached only through intellect, then where would the brain-damaged, the mentally retarded, the little child be? When Jesus put the little child in the midst of His disciples, He did not tell the little child to become like His disciples; He told the disciples to become like the little child. And some of the greatest intellects of the ages—Saint Augustine, Blaise Pascal, G.K. Chesterton, C.S. Lewis, and countless others—have all had to come the same way, in simple, childlike faith.

How like God!

❧ Reflections

RUTH HAD A CRISIS OF FAITH, not unlike many of our experiences. We want to have someone prove that God is real. That He loves us. It is a request He always answers, "Yes, my child, I will prove to you I am real. I want you to know Me. Only have faith, step out and know that My everlasting arms of love will catch you."

When we do, we have the glorious, unexpected blessing of seeing Him reveal Himself. It may be in a way we could never have imagined, or in a way so simple we can't believe we didn't see it before. Oh, the unlimited creativity of God. He can do anything He wants.

Is your faith weak or strong today? Do you need God to prove His validity or are you basking in the absolute knowledge of His close presence? Regardless, God is real.

Journal

❦ Journal

Do not be anxious about anything, but in everything, by prayer and petition, with thanksgiving, present your requests to God.

PHILIPPIANS 4:6

A Bed For Jasper

D.J. Note

Jasper needed a bed to call his own. "A regular old cardboard box just isn't good enough," my daughter told me. She suggested we invest in a soft, over-stuffed circular model, with a convenient cutout entrance for her apricot-colored tabby.

"A store-bought pet-bed could be expensive, Monica," I explained. "And it's possible Jasper might refuse to sleep in it anyway."

"But Mom-m-m, Jasper deserves a bed of his own," she insisted. "He's special. P-l-e-a-s-e, Mom."

The plea in her large, slate blue eyes reminded me of the special place Jasper held in her heart.

Since his arrival on Christmas Eve, Monica found Jasper a willing participant in afternoon tea parties of dry cat food and water. He appeared to enjoy the mid-morning rides in her bright-pink baby doll stroller. And tolerating her doll's blue and white plaid bonnet and cotton flannel nightie was worth all the home-spun attention Monica lavished on him.

"Let's drive to the store and see what we can find," I suggested. "They have lots of boxes. Maybe it would be wise just to try a cardboard box first."

On the way to the market, I suggested we pray. "You do not have, because you do not ask . . ." I said, flashing a smile her way.

"Lord, You know just the right bed for Jasper," Monica whispered, "Please help us find it."

The middle-aged clerk wore a large full-length white apron and a friendly smile. Returning his hearty grin, I explained what we were looking for.

"I'll just take a look in the back," he said to Monica, tilting his glasses to focus through his bifocals. Then he hurried away to the storeroom in search of a box.

Monica's waning smile revealed her doubt about the store clerk's mission. But when he returned, we both stood in disbelief at the lovely wooden box he held in his hands. The helpful gentleman couldn't possibly have known the label pasted at one end of the box was God's perfect answer to our prayer.

Amidst luscious grapes, yellow melons, and sparkling sapphire-colored berries, the word JASPER extended across the entire sticker, in bold red letters. Underneath, tiny print advertised "California's Finest Fruits."

"Ask, and ye shall receive . . ." I laughed.

"Oh my gosh!" Monica squealed. Wrapping her arms around my waist she repeated, "Thank you, Jesus! Thank you."

The clerk raised his thinning eyebrows over our giddy reaction to a plain wooden box.

"The box is for her kitty." Pausing briefly, I added, "His name is Jasper! How much do I owe you?" I asked, digging through my purse for my worn-out wallet.

"Nothing at all. It's yours," he smiled.

We offered another round of gratitude to the sweet gentleman God had used to show us His love.

I threw my arm around Monica's shoulder, and with our box in tow, we giggled our way out of the store. Jasper had his perfect bed.

An unexpected miracle? Maybe. A coincidence? Never.

A blessing? Absolutely.

❧ *Reflections*

DOES GOD CARE EVEN ABOUT A BED for a cat? Does the Lord God Almighty who lives in heaven and sees the whole earth care about a designer bed with a cat's name on it? A name that few cats have? D.J. and Monica can answer a resounding, "Yes!" Our God cares even about a bed for a cat. If that is so, He cares about everything that you and I are facing. Therefore, why should we worry or fret? God is in control. He'll provide a cat's bed and everything we need to go through our difficulty or struggle.

Do your concerns seem too small to take to God? Does it seem like you'll only bother Him? Nothing is too small for God's loving touch. Take it to Him, He wants to work—and it may be in an unexpected way.

Journal

❧ Journal

Be devoted to one another . . . Honor one another . . .

ROMANS 12:10

The Blessing Of Affirmation: Let's Celebrate!

Lynell Gray

I CELEBRATE THE UNIQUELY HUMAN ABILITY to celebrate—to ritualize affirmations of our most significant events and deeply held values. I am a big celebrator, a sentimental seeker of ways and reasons to celebrate.

My three children are more like my husband, too busy and too practical to commit much time or energy to celebrations, although they are kind enough to participate more or less cooperatively in the many celebrations I have planned for our family through the years.

Our oldest daughter, though, has the potential to be a celebrator par excellence. I know this because of a certain Mother's Day, about five years ago, when Christina was in high school.

I was feeling shell-shocked that year, suffering from post-traumatic stress syndrome before the trauma of mothering three teenagers was even close to being over. I felt shaken, off-balance, unanchored in a very big, unknown sea, which I had come to feel completely unqualified to navigate. I no longer knew how to be a mother. It had been a very rough year.

I awoke that Mother's Day morning with a feeling of dread. I had never felt more like burrowing under the bedding and never coming out. But when I finally opened my door, there was Christina, grinning in triumph, her eyes glistening faintly with tears.

My firstborn had artistically laid down a "carpet" of white

sheets winding down the hallway, through the family room and kitchen to the dining room. On it she had scattered hundreds of fresh pink rose petals from our own bushes, which had perfumed the air with their deep scent. She took my arm and escorted me to the breakfast table, where my husband had waffles and strawberry butter waiting. It was a conspiracy of love.

I had never felt more grateful to be the mother of such a child, and never more successful in the job, as I did at that moment. I will never forget the unexpected blessing of that Mother's Day and its essential message of hope.

Yes, I love celebrations, and I continue to create them. But I never expect to top the celebration of the mother-daughter bond which Christina engineered with such sensitivity and flair one Mother's Day, an era ago, when she let me know, without words, that I was a mother worth celebrating.

Now every Mother's Day, in my mind I am crowned once again Queen of Mothers amidst a swirl of white bed sheets and pink rose petals, and through my incredulous tears I see Christina, one of three amazing God-breathed blessings—my babies all grown taller and stronger and more beautiful than I can say.

ᴥᴤ *Reflections*

WHETHER WE ARE RAISING TEENAGERS OR NOT, we often feel shell-shocked by life's problems and difficulties. When discouragement is overwhelming us, God steps forth to encourage our hearts and let us know we are appreciated. Lynell certainly never expected God to work in the way He did through Christina's loving actions. Lynell's experience can also be a lesson to us of how important it is for us to reach out and show our love to others. It may have been that Christina didn't fully comprehend the incredible impact she would have on her mother that Mother's Day. But her actions had a powerful effect and brought an unexpected blessing to one mother's heart. We need to bless others in similar ways.

Has God been prompting you to demonstrate your love for someone in an unexpected way? Don't delay, obey Him now. It will bless them and you.

Journal

❧ Journal

*Praise be to the God and Father of our Lord
Jesus Christ, the Father of compassion and
the God of all comfort, who comforts us in all
our troubles, so that we can comfort those in
any trouble with the comfort we ourselves
have received from God.*

II Corinthians 1:3, 4

Unexpected Prayer Ministry

Dr. James Dobson

M Y WIFE, SHIRLEY, did not grow up in a Christian home, and her experiences were very different from mine. Her father was an alcoholic who abused his family and spoke of God only when cursing. Shirley's mother, while not a Christian, was a wonderful woman who loved her two children. She recognized her need for assistance in raising her kids and began sending them to a neighborhood evangelical church when they were very young. There, Shirley learned about Jesus and she learned to pray.

This little girl, trapped in poverty and the heartache of alcoholism, began talking to the Lord about her family. Especially after her parents were divorced, she asked Him to grant two requests. First, she prayed for a Christian stepfather who would love and provide for them. Second, Shirley knew she wanted to have a godly home and family someday. She began asking the Lord for a Christian husband when the time came to marry. It touches my heart today to think about that child, alone on her knees in her bedroom, talking to God about her need. I was out there somewhere oblivious of her existence, but the Lord had me in a long-term training program. By the time I met this pretty young lady in college, I did not have to be pushed.

That story beautifully illustrates the efficacy of prayer. The great God of the universe, with all His majesty and power, was not too busy to hear the small voice of a child in need. He not only brought the two of us together, but He sent a fine, never-married man to be Shirley's new stepfather. Both her parents are Christians today and are serving the Lord in their community.

When Shirley and I met and fell in love, therefore, we each brought a strong faith to the relationship. From those early days, we determined that Jesus Christ would have the preeminent place in our lives. I remember the two of us sitting in my junky old Mercury before we were married and expressing a prayer of dedication for our future home. We asked the Lord to direct our paths, and especially, to put His blessing on any children He might loan to us. Then I pledged to Shirley that I would spend the rest of my life trying to provide the kind of happiness and security she had missed as a child. This was the foundation on which our little family was built.

Now, after more than three decades together, we have seen God's consistent faithfulness in response to our prayers. I don't know where we would be without this source of strength and sustenance. In fact, the most significant development of our marriage has been the growth and maturation of Shirley's prayer life. She has become what is sometimes called a "prayer warrior," maintaining a constant communion with the Lord. It is fitting, given this spiritual fervor, that she has been appointed chairman of the National Day of Prayer.

❧ *Reflections*

As Jim and Shirley's story exemplifies, God doesn't waste anything. He takes the broken pieces of our lives and puts together unique blends of ministry. He picks up the puzzle pieces of our lives and forms a foundation of strength that blesses others. With His creativity, sovereignty, and wisdom, He can take anything we offer Him and fashion a blessing from it. We may have trouble believing that's possible while we're in the midst of pain or little hope. Shirley could never have imagined God's unexpected plan of blessing. But God knew all along and He never doubted His ability to bring it to pass. He knows what He has planned for you and me. It will be designed uniquely from the broken puzzle pieces we place in His capable hands.

❧

Have you seen God's plan come together yet? If not, don't give up. He will bring it to pass.

Journal

❧ Journal

_____

_____

_____

_____

_____

_____

_____

_____

_____

_____

_____

_____

_____

_____

_____

_____

_____

_____

_____

_____

_____

_____

*My grace is sufficient for you, for my power
is made perfect in weakness.*

II Corinthians 12:9

God's Miraculous Grace

Libby C. Carpenter

AFTER A RESTLESS NIGHT of little sleep and much worry, I awoke to face a day I feared . . . another trip to the hospital to visit my ailing father in a nearby city. Dad had been admitted a week earlier with a heart problem. Then yesterday the doctors had given us no hope for his recovery. I felt alone and in despair.

As I pulled onto a crowded interstate highway to begin the twenty-five mile drive to the hospital, I poured out my heart to God. At first argumentative, I questioned, "Why? Surely something could be done to save my father!" After much pleading, somehow I managed to pray, "God, there is nothing I can do. I put my earthly father in Your hands."

At that moment I caught a glimpse of a light gray tractor trailer in my rear view mirror. As the truck passed, and merged in front of me, I spotted huge, black letters on the back of the trailer. Through my tears I read the word G-R-A-C-E. I fixed my eyes on the bold inscription and followed the truck to the hospital exit. As I drove, all the worry and anxiety I had felt in recent days faded away, replaced with God's peace. What a blessing to know God cared enough for me to place the truck in my path, assuring me His grace would be sufficient.

That night when my brother called to inform me of Dad's passing, my tears returned, but this time with the comforting reassurance that by God's miraculous grace my father had entered the Church Triumphant!

✥ Reflections

GOD'S GRACE IS SUFFICIENT. It is not only sufficient, it is abundant. There is never too little to take care of our needs. Libby will never forget how God unexpectedly reminded her of that truth. He would empower her to face her father's passing into eternity. Many people may have noticed the name of "GRACE" on that truck as it passed on the highway, but it didn't have the special meaning for them that it did for Libby. God intended it to be an unexpected blessing for a hurting heart. He will do whatever it takes to come to our rescue, comfort and guide us, because He loves us with an everlasting love.

✥

How have you seen God's grace be sufficient? Praise Him for His abundant provision.

✑ Journal

Journal

✥ Journal

_____

_____

_____

_____

_____

_____

_____

_____

_____

_____

_____

_____

_____

_____

_____

_____

_____

_____

_____

_____

_____

Trust in him at all times, O people; pour out
your heart to him, for God is our refuge.

PSALM 62:8

Our Unexpected Blessing

Esther L. Vogt

O<small>N</small> S<small>ATURDAY</small>, D<small>ECEMBER</small> 10, 1949, the long hours of labor finally ended when our son Ranney Lee was born. My delivery had been extremely difficult, for Dr. Janzen was forced to do an extraction/inversion. Still, we were happy to receive our son, as was his sister, Shirley. But our joy was short-lived.

"Your baby is very ill," the doctor told us. "Due to the difficult birth he has suffered brain damage. It's just a matter of time . . ." His voice faded.

I stared dismally at the Christmas lights that blinked on and off at the south end of the old hospital corridor, and I felt like shutting my ears to the strains of "Joy To The World" drifting down the halls. Joy? It seemed a mockery.

Shirley told her Sunday school teacher on Sunday: "I had a baby brother last night, but I think he's going to be with Jesus!"

On Monday the nurse rustled into my room and laid the tiny blanketed bundle into my arms without a word. Obviously I was given a chance to hold my son while I could. As he moaned and whimpered, my tears dripped on his pain-wracked face. How could he possibly survive? I cried, "Lord, I can't bear to see him suffer so. Please take him home!" I prayed only that it might be over soon.

Tuesday morning the doctor bounced into my room and seated himself by my bed. "I don't know what's happened, Esther, but your son is very much better today. It's the grace of God!" Our hopes soared. After 30 days we took Ranney home.

As a victim of cerebral palsy, he struggled. He couldn't sit alone until he was two, feed himself until he was six, and didn't walk until he was ten, but his mind was keen and sharp. He developed normally in every other way.

I wheeled him to public school on his three-wheeled bike daily, and in spite of his cramped fingers, he kept up with his studies. He had a great sense of humor and made many friends who scooted him from class to class.

When he was eight, he accepted Christ, and at age twelve, our pastor baptized him upon his confession of faith. After he successfully completed the eighth grade, he was ready for high school. But at first our administration balked.

"With the rush and bustle along the halls, he'll get knocked down," the principal said. "But we'll give him six weeks!" Yet he was amazed at Ranney's congenial personality, his love for people, and his keen grasp for learning. We were delighted when he graduated from high school with honors! "He earned his grades," Mr. Klassen announced proudly at commencement.

Ranney enrolled at Emporia State University (geared for the handicapped) as a business major and music minor. In 1973 he graduated from the business department with honors. After graduation, the school offered him a job as statistician for Dining Services, and provided him with his own computer. By now he was in a wheelchair. After seventeen years, he was laid off his job but took it as of the Lord, for he'd often wished for more time for Bible study.

He always had a deep love for music but couldn't use his cramped fingers on the keyboard. Then he invested in a "music program" for his computer—which miraculously "writes" his music down on paper. In the past seven years, he has "written" his own music and taped his copious arrangements of hymns, plus secular songs. His best-known arrangement is "What A Friend We Have In Jesus." In spite of his handicap, he has been a great blessing to many people—as a person, musician, and even in serving as a deacon in his church.

As I think back how gravely ill he was at birth and our prayers for the Lord to release him, I realize now God had a plan for him—a unexpected plan only He knew.

Today we praise God that He knew how to bring blessings into our lives through Ranney.

Reflections

ESTHER COULD NEVER HAVE ANTICIPATED that her prayers for her son's life would be answered in such a unique way. God knew His great plans for that baby. When we are faced with challenges that make us cry out to God, our faith may seem small. But God, in His understanding tenderness, takes our groaning and weaves them into the fabric of His will. Each strand has different colors and a unique relationship with the other strands around it. God knows how to make that fabric look whole and complete—an unexpected blessing—even with so many different strands being used.

Are the strands of your life seemingly jumbled? They may seem to be in disarray, but God knows the plan for His glory with each strand.

✒ Journal

_____

_____

_____

_____

_____

_____

_____

_____

_____

_____

_____

_____

_____

_____

_____

_____

_____

_____

_____

_____

_____

Journal

Let us then approach the throne of grace with
confidence, so that we may receive mercy and
find grace to help us in our time of need.

HEBREWS 4:16

The Power
Of Prayer

Dr. David Jeremiah

Goᴅ ɪs ᴀʟᴡᴀʏs ᴜᴘ ᴛᴏ sᴏᴍᴇᴛʜɪɴɢ. You've got to trust Him. I was reminded of this the other day when I saw the following true story reported by a worker with the Overseas Missionary Fellowship: (based on the missionary's presentation at a church in Michigan).

While serving at a small field hospital in Africa, I traveled every two weeks by bicycle through the jungle to a nearby city for supplies. This required camping overnight halfway. On one of these trips, I saw two men fighting in the city. One was seriously hurt so I treated him and witnessed to him about the Lord Jesus Christ. I then returned home without incident.

Upon arriving in the city several weeks later, I was approached by the man I had treated earlier. He told me he had known that I carried money and medicine. He said, "Some friends and I followed you into the jungle, knowing you would camp overnight. We waited for you to go to sleep and planned to kill you and take your money and drugs. Just as we were about to move into your campsite, we saw that you were surrounded by 26 armed guards."

I laughed at this and said, "I was certainly all alone out in the jungle campsite."

The young man pressed the point, "No sir, I was not the only one to see the guards. My five friends also saw them, and we all counted them. It was because of those guards that we were afraid and left you alone."

At this point of my church presentation in Michigan, one of

the men in the church stood up and interrupted me. He asked, "Can you tell me the exact date when this happened?"

I thought for awhile and recalled the date.

The man in the congregation then gave his side of the story. He stated, "On that night in Africa it was day here. I was preparing to play golf. As I put my bags in the car, I felt the Lord leading me to pray for you. In fact, the urging was so great that I called the men of this church together to pray for you. Will all those men who met to pray please stand?"

The men who had met that day to pray together stood . . . there were 26 of them!

❧ Reflections

DAVID JEREMIAH'S STORY reminds us of the power of prayer and the fact that God's nudgings to pray are important and real. Wonder if that man hadn't been prayed for? Might he even be alive today? Although that church member did hear the results of his faithfulness to pray and his enlistment of twenty-five men to pray with him, you and I may not always hear the results of our prayers. But that doesn't mean God didn't use them. We may not know until we reach heaven. Won't that be a great time of rejoicing in seeing the power of our prayers? Let's respond to every nudging God gives us to pray for others.

The next time God nudges you to pray, will you? By faith know that He will make your prayers effective.

Journal

Journal

❦ Contributors

Patricia A.J. Allen is the wife of a fully recovered husband. Her recently married son has a lovely wife. Patricia dreams of her own furniture design house. With God all things are possible. Contact: 1848 ENC 10, Newton, NC 28658.

Marie Asner is a church musician/writer/workshop presenter in Overland Park, KS. Marie has been nominated for the Kansas Governor's Art Award, Mary Roberts Rinehart Award in Poetry, and the Athena Award in Mentoring.

Ellen Bergh began writing after graduating college at 45. She has published inspirational meditations, disability newsletters, personality profiles, book reviews, and technical manuals. She facilitates The Antelope Valley Christian Writers Guild. Contact: mastermedia@hughes.net.

Delores Elaine Bius has sold over 1,800 articles and stories in 26 years of writing. She is an instructor for American Christian Writers and speaks at conferences and retreats. She is a widow and mother of five sons. Contact: 6400 So. Narragansett Ave., Chicago, IL 60638. (773) 586-4384.

Kitty Bucholtz, President of the Tempe Christian Writers Club, has also been published in *God's Abundance*. She writes devotionals, articles, and is currently working on a novel. Contact: P.O. Box 68114, Phoenix, AZ 85082-8114. jkbuch@primenet.com.

Penelope Carlevato has been married to Norm for 34 years, has three grown children and five grandchildren, plus a degree in Nursing. She has a love of tea and writing. Also, Marie speaks on sharing God's love over a cup of tea. Contact: teatime@eni.net.

Libby C. Carpenter is a former teacher, wife of Hugh, mother of two, and grandmother of three. Active in Bethel Lutheran Church, she enjoys reading, gardening, and researching family history. Contact: 426 Aderholdt Road, Lincolnton, NC 28092. (704) 435-2932.

Laura Chalk is a 1991 graduate of the University of Kansas, with a bachelor of arts degree in English. She is a stay-at-home mother with two boys, ages six and four. Contact: chalkchat@juno.com.

Joan Clayton is a published author. She has written five books and over 300 published articles. She is also the Religion Columnist for her local newspaper. She and her husband, Emmitt, are retired educators and reside in Portales, New Mexico.

Doris C. Crandall is an inspirational writer who lives with her husband Richard. An award-winning writer, Doris' articles have been published in many inspirational and religious magazines. Contact: 2303 Victoria Street, Amarillo, TX 79106. Rcrand1068@aol.com.

Lille Diane is a sought after speaker and vocalist for groups, seminars, and retreats nationwide. Her inspiring story "From Ashes to Beauty" transforms lives, young and old. Contact: P.O. Box 924, Oakview, CA 93022. (805) 649-1805.

Maria Faulconer is a freelance writer, teacher, and therapist. She has authored

Maria Faulconer is a freelance writer, teacher, and therapist. She has authored a children's book, *Arianna and the Strawberry Tea*. Her inspirational articles have appeared in a variety of newspapers and magazines, among them *Brio* and *St. Anthony Messenger*. Contact: TBVZ10B@prodigy.com.

Nancy L. Goodwin, freelance writer, is married and the mother of two. She is a lover of words with a desire to communicate God's words of love. Contact: 64555 Falcon Lane, Cambridge, OH 43725. (614) 439-3512. Nanwrite@mailexcite.com 33150.

Lynell Gray is a freelance writer and elementary schoolteacher. She has authored professional materials for teachers as well as inspirational articles and poems. Contact: 2867 Balfore St. Riverside, CA 92506. (909) 788-2638.

Sharon Hanby-Robie ASID interior designer for 20 years, now an author, speaker, TV personality, and Creative Director for Starburst Publishers. Contact: sharonrobie@starburstpublishers.com.

Bonnie Compton Hanson, writer/speaker, is co-author of three books plus hundreds of published poems and articles. Contact: 3330 S. Lowell St., Santa Ana, CA 92707. (714) 751-7824. bonnieh1@ix.netcom.com.

Diana L. James, author of *Bounce Back, You Can Bounce Back, Too*, and numerous published articles, speaks for conferences, retreats, seminars, and Christian women's groups. She was a TV interview host for five years. Contact: (714) 457-1213. DianaJames@aol.com.

Pauline Jaramillo is a journalist and freelance writer. Some of her published work include: short stories; personal experience, research, and profile articles; one-act plays; poetry. Some of her work has been published in Braille. Contact: P.O. Box 225, Rim Forest, CA 92378. (909) 337-7032.

Karen Kosman worked as a medical assistant for fifteen years. Now, as a freelance writer, she works for the Great Physician. Many diverse life experiences allow her to write and speak on how God heals the hurting heart.

Tina Krause is an award-winning newspaper columnist, public speaker, and freelance writer of over 650 columns, magazine articles, and feature stories. She is the wife of Jim, mother of two, and grandmother of Ian James. Contact: 223 Abington St., Valparaiso, IN 46385. tinak@netnitco.net.

Janice L. Krouskop, MPH, RD is the author of *Happy Thoughts for a Healthy Life*. She speaks professionally providing inspiration at conferences, retreats, and seminars. Contact: 218 Timber Ridge Rd, Pittsburgh, PA 15238. (412) 967-9683. jankrd@aol.com.

Georgia Curtis Ling is an entertaining speaker, writer, and newspaper columnist, who touches the heart and tickles the funny bone as she shares stories about faith, love, and life. She is published in numerous magazines, and newspapers. She's appeared in four of the *God's Vitamin "C" for the Spirit* series, and *God's Abundance*. Contact: 4716 W. Glenhaven Drive, Everett, WA 98203. (425) 257-0377.

Gail Gaymer Martin is a professional licensed counselor and instructor of English at Detroit College of Business. She is a speaker and freelance writer with five books and sixty published articles and short stories. Contact: 27335 Eldorado Place, Lathrup Village, MI 48076. martinga@aol.com.

Kathy Collard Miller is the author of 30 books including the best-selling *God's Vitamin "C" for the Spirit* and *God's Abundance*. She speaks across the nation and internationally. Contact: P.O. Box 1058, Placentia, CA 92871. (714) 993-2654. Kathyspeak@aol.com.

Patricia R. Mora is married to illustrator Al Mora. They have one son and two granddaughters. She desires to help women grow in serving their families and their community in Christ. She lives in Olathe, KS. Contact: (913) 393-2103. Bluelantern@juno.com.

Lynn D. Morrissey, *Words of Life Ministries* founder, professional writer and speaker, specializes in workshops on prayer-journaling, spiritual autobiographies, discovering gifts/missions, writing, women's topics, volunteer management, and original speeches upon request. Contact: 155 Linden Ave., St. Louis, MO 63105. (314) 727-8137.

Sharyn McDonald works full time for Evangelical Christian Credit Union and lives in Garden Grove, California with husband Darrell and their three college-aged children. She is active in her church and in ministry to women.

Mary Beth Nelson lives with her husband in Clarendon, Texas. She is a retired elementary teacher and freelance writer. Her family consists of four children and nine grandchildren. Her hobbies are music and gardening.

D.J. Note is a wife, mother of two teenagers, a Mom's-In-Touch leader and full-time freelance writer. Her love of God, family, and country life inspire her writing. Contact: 9821 Hwy. 62, Eagle Point, OR 97524. (541) 826-3471. djnote@juno.com.

Rhonda Wheeler Stock has been married for 15 years, has four children, ages 4-14. Born and reared in Kansas City, MO, and graduated from University of Missouri, Columbia. She writes and speaks to women's and youth groups. Contact: 9336 Greenway Ln., Lenexa, KS 66215. (913) 492-9607. RhondaWS@juno.com.

Rebecca Thesman works at home as a homemaker/writer. Her interests include family, Bible study, cooking, writing, and teaching. She and husband Bob, have been married 22 years and have one son, Caleb, one dog, Rocky, and one cat, Ivory.

Bob Turnbull is a national conference speaker, former actor, author of eight books, including *Marriage Mentors* with wife, Yvonne, and is the founder of the Waikiki Beach Chaplaincy. He has won five Angels at the Excellence in Media Awards. Contact: P.O. Box 4170, Mission Viejo, CA 92690. (714) 457-1410.

Esther L. Vogt is a widow with three grown children and three grandchildren. She is an author of 24 published fiction books, mostly historical novels. Contact: 113 South Ash, Hillsboro, KS 67063. (316) 947-3796.

Jan Woodard enjoys speaking for inspirational audiences and encouraging other writers. A wife, mom, and prize-winning writer for *Guideposts* and other publications, she's convinced every day is an adventure in grace. Contact: 270 Sunset Dr., Indiana, PA 15701. (724) 465-5886.

Susan Kimmel Wright lives in an old farmhouse with her husband, three children, and assorted animals. She has written many articles and a children's mystery book series (Herald Press). Contact: 221 Fawcett Church Rd., Bridgeville, PA 15017-1512. (412) 746-2517.

Jeanne Zornes speaks and writes with humor and compassion on encouragement and perseverance. Widely published, her latest book is *When I Got on the Highway to Heaven, I Didn't Expect Rocky Roads* (Shaw). Contact: 1025 Meeks, Wenatchee, WA 98801.

❧ Credits

Self Worth Restored adapted from *Joy That Lasts* by Gary Smalley with Al Janssen, Zondervan, MI, 1986. Used by permission.

The Building of a Prayer Ministry adapted from *When God Doesn't Make Sense* by James Dobson, Tyndale, IL, 1993. Used by permission.

The Power of Prayer from *PRAYER: The Great Adventure* by Dr. David Jeremiah, Multnomah, OR, 1997. Used by permission.

The Deal of a Lifetime from *The Wonderful Spirit Filled Life*, by Charles Stanley, Thomas Nelson Publishers, TN, 1992. Used by permission.

Unexpected Protection from *Stress Fractures* by Charles Swindoll, Multnomah, OR, 1990. Used by permission.

Expressing Needed Love from *The Father Connection* by Josh McDowell, Broadman & Holman, TN, 1996. Used by permission.

The Noble Spork from *Secret Strength* by Joni Eareckson Tada, Multnomah, OR. Used by permission.

Unexpected Praise adapted from *Over the Top* by Zig Ziglar, Thomas Nelson, TN, 1994. Used by permission.

Blessing of Truth from *Who You Are When No One's Looking* by Bill Hybels, IVP, IL, 1987. Used by permission.

Unexpected Faith, *It's My Turn* by Ruth Bell Graham, Fleming H. Revell, MI, 1982. Used by permission.

Unexpected Gratitude and *Unexpected Sacrifice* adapted from *Six Hours One Friday* by Max Lucado, Multnomah, OR, 1989. Used by permission.

Unexpected Emotions from *Normal Is Just a Setting On Your Dryer* by Patsy Clairmont Focus on the Family, CO, 1993. Used by permission.

Expert Credentials for an Unexpected Ministry from *Fresh Elastic for Stretched Out Moms* by Barbara Johnson, Fleming H. Revell, MI, 1986. Used by permission.

Every Problem Will Change You from *Tough Times Never Last, but Tough People Do!* by Robert H. Schuller, Thomas Nelson Publishers, TN, 1986.

The Unexpected Blessings of Sacrifice from *The Secret of Happiness* by Billy Graham, Doubleday & Company, Inc., New York, 1955.

Books by Starburst Publishers

(Partial listing—full list available on request)
www.starburstpublishers.com

God's Unexpected Blessings
—Edited by Kathy Collard Miller

Learn to see the Unexpected Blessings in life. Individual essays about experiences that on the surface appear to be only bad or negative, but in the end, God used for something good whether in our own lives or through us to benefit another. Witness God at work in our lives. Learn to trust God in action. Realize that we always have a choice to learn and benefit from these experiences by letting God prove His promise of turning all things for our good.

(hardcover) ISBN 0914984071 **$18.95**

God's Abundance
—Edited by Kathy Collard Miller

This day-by-day inspirational is a collection of thoughts by leading Christian writers such as, Patsy Clairmont, Jill Briscoe, Liz Curtis Higgs, and Naomi Rhode. *God's Abundance* is based on God's Word for a simpler, yet more abundant life. Most people think more about the future while the present passes through their hands. Learn to make all aspects of your life—personal, business, financial, relationships, even housework can be a "spiritual abundance of simplicity."

(hardcover) ISBN 0914984977 **$19.95**

Revelation—God's Word for the Biblically-Inept
—Daymond R. Duck

Revelation—God's Word for the Biblically-Inept is the first in a new series designed to make understanding and learning the Bible as easy and fun as learning your ABC's. Reading the Bible is one thing, understanding it is another! This book breaks down the barrier of difficulty and helps take the Bible off the pedestal and into your hands.

(trade paper) ISBN 0914984985 **$16.95**

Daniel—God's Word for the Biblically-Inept
—Daymond R. Duck

Daniel is the second book in the *God's Word for the Biblically-Inept* series designed to make understanding and learning the Bible easy and fun. *Daniel* is a book of prophecy and the key to understanding the mysteries of the Tribulation and End-Time events. This book is broken down into bite-sized pieces making it easy to comprehend and incorporate into your daily life.

(trade paper) ISBN 0914984489 **$16.95**

Conversations With God the Father
—Mark R. Littleton

Subtitled: *Encounters with the One True God*. If you are greatly interested in improving your fellowship with God and want to know what He is like, then this book will help by presenting answers to questions as God might answer them, while painting a powerful portrait of His personality.

(hardcover) ISBN 0914984195 **$17.95**

God Is!
—Mark R. Littleton

"Heart-Tugging" inspirational stories, quotes & illustrations that will leave a powerful mental and emotional impact on the reader. Short and easy-to-read sketches, embracing the attributes of God, will inspire your spirit and brighten your day. Topics include, God Is Love, God Is Good, God Is Wise, and more.

(hardcover) ISBN 0914984926 **$14.95**

If I Only Knew . . . What Would Jesus Do?
—Joan Hake Robie

In what direction are you walking? Is it in His direction? And what about what you're saying? Would He say it? *If I Only Knew . . .* is designed with timely questions, poignant answers, and Scripture. When confronted with a nasty situation—stop and think—*What Would Jesus Do?*

(trade paper)   ISBN   091498439X   **$9.95**

God's Vitamin "C" for the Spirit
—Kathy Collard Miller & D. Larry Miller

Subtitled: *"Tug-at-the-Heart" Stories to Fortify and Enrich Your Life.* Includes inspiring stories and anecdotes that emphasize Christian ideals and values by Barbara Johnson, Billy Graham, Nancy L. Dorner, Dave Dravecky, Patsy Clairmont, Charles Swindoll, H. Norman Wright, Adell Harvey, Max Lucado, James Dobson, Jack Hayford and many other well-known Christian speakers and writers. Topics include: Love, Family Life, Faith and Trust, Prayer, Marriage, Relationships, Grief, Spiritual Life, Perseverance, Christian Living, and God's Guidance.

(trade paper)   ISBN   0914984837   **$12.95**

God's Vitamin "C" for the Hurting Spirit
—Kathy Collard Miller & D. Larry Miller

The latest in the best-selling God's Vitamin "C" for the Spirit series, this collection of real-life stories expresses the breadth and depth of God's love for us in our times of need. Rejuvenating and inspiring thoughts from some of the most-loved Christian writers such as Max Lucado, Cynthia Heald, Gary Smalley, and Barbara Johnson. Topics include: Death, Divorce/Separation, Financial Loss, and Physical Illness.

(trade paper)   ISBN   0914984691   **$12.95**

God's Vitamin "C" for the Spirit of WOMEN
—Kathy Collard Miller

Subtitled: "Tug-at-the Heart" stories to Inspire and Delight Your Spirit. A beautiful treasury of timeless stories, quotes and poetry designed by and for women. Well-known Christian women like Liz Curtis Higgs, Pasty Clairmont, Naomi Rhode and Elisabeth Elliott share from their hearts on subjects like Marriage, Motherhood, Christian Living, Faith and Friendship.

(trade paper)   ISBN   0914984934   **$12.95**

A Woman's Guide To Spiritual Power
—Nancy L. Dorner

Subtitled: Through Scriptural Prayer. Do your prayers seem to go "against a brick wall?" Does God sometimes seem far away or non-existent? If your answer is "Yes," you are not alone. Prayer must be the cornerstone of your relationship to God. "This book is a powerful tool for anyone who is serious about prayer and discipleship."—Florence Littauer

(trade paper)   ISBN   0914984470   **$9.95**

Purchasing Information:
www.starburstpublishers.com

Books are available from your favorite bookstore, either from current stock or special order. To assist bookstore in locating your selection be sure to give title, author, and ISBN #. If unable to purchase from the bookstore you may order direct from STARBURST PUBLISHERS. When ordering enclose full payment plus $3.00 for shipping and handling ($4.00 if Canada or overseas). Payment in U.S. Funds only. Please allow two to three weeks minimum (longer overseas) for delivery. Make checks payable to and mail to: STARBURST PUBLISHERS, P.O. Box 4123, LANCASTER, PA 17604. Credit card orders may also be placed by calling 1-800-441-1456 (credit card orders only), Mon-Fri, 8:30 a.m.—5:30 p.m. Eastern Time. Prices subject to change without notice. Catalog available for a 9 x 12 self-addressed envelope with 4 first-class stamps.